THE GREAT LOVERS
COOKBOOK

May 1990

Laura and Bruce!

We wish you
The most delicious
times together!
Congratulations
in love & marriage.

Fondly,
Lisa & Ray

THE GREAT LOVERS
COOKBOOK

BY
SUSAN HARTZ &
KATHLEEN KENT

bp

First Printing: September, 1984

Published by Betterway Publications, Inc.
White Hall, VA 22987

Cover design and illustration by G.B. MacIntosh © 1984
Book illustrations by Charles Peale © 1984
Typography by Graphic Communications, Inc.

Library of Congress Cataloging in Publication Data

Hartz, Susan
   The great lovers cookbook.

   Includes index.
   1. Cookery, International.   I. Kent, Kathleen
II. Title.   III. Title: Lovers cookbook.
TX725.A1H29   1984   641.59   84-14625
ISBN 0-932620-38-8 (pbk.)

Printed in the United States of America

To
the ones we love

CONTENTS

INTRODUCTION

In this age of high technology and super sophistication we are confident there are still those individuals who believe in and even seek out a touch of romance in their lives. It is for those people we have written this book.

Everyone is enchanted by a love story. The astounding growth in popularity of romantic fiction during the last few years confirms this. History also attests to it. Every period offers us examples of famous lovers. Sometimes the love between two people transcends their own time and becomes legendary. It is to those "great lovers" that we have dedicated our efforts.

We have looked back at famous pairs of lovers: real, legendary, and fictional. Some are tragic. Some are notorious. Some are magnificent. Some are well documented in the literature of their time or have been a source of inspiration for poets, dramatists, and musicians. But all, in one way or another, have become larger than life.

How then, you ask, does all this resolve itself into a cookbook? There is an easy answer to that question. Food, the preparing of it, and the sharing of it, is an exciting part of any relationship. It becomes even more meaningful when the meal is to be shared with someone special. After all, isn't dining one of the foremost courting rituals of all time?

Our collection of romantic diners begins 3,000 years ago. From that point in time we have chosen from lovers throughout the centuries. . .until the 1940's. Our only limitation was to be sure that all those lovers chosen were no longer living. (No lawsuits, thank you.) Thus the absence of any contemporary pairs.

Coincidentally our choice of famous lovers has resulted in an exciting

montage of cuisines from around the world. We suggest menus and provide instructions for preparation of foods from the Middle East, Europe,
the Orient, and the United States. In every case we have attempted to
capture the essence of the moment for the two famous people.

We are by no means stating emphatically that a particular pair of lovers
shared the meal we describe. We have looked at the time period in which
the lovers lived, considered what foods were available and what might
have been favorites for each of them. Inspired by what we learned, we
created a menu for each pair. Then we wove a fantasy around them,
sometimes with a suggestion of a setting, sometimes with a stretch of the
imagination. What we hope we have portrayed is a real sense of the
spellbinding aura of immortal love.

We invite you to indulge yourself in a fantastic smorgasbord of food and
love, fact and fiction. Be adventurous. Here is a chance to experience the
past, to capture the wonder and the magic of a moment in time where
famous lovers have dallied and dined. The province of love is boundless.
The means to share your affection is only as far away as your kitchen.
Laugh together, have fun together, love together. After all, you may be
famous lovers someday, too!

SOLOMON
AND
SHEBA

In the sun-drenched city of Jerusalem, almost three thousand years ago, two noble monarchs met. He was a king named Solomon. She was a queen called Sheba. One was wise; the other mysterious.

Since that legendary meeting their names have been linked through the ages. Their story spirals down the centuries recounted in the Old Testament, Arabic legend, and Ethiopian history. According to tradition, the queen is supposed to have traveled a great distance in a caravan laden with riches to honor the mighty King of Israel. Whereupon the king, charmed by her intelligence and beauty, welcomed her as an equal.

In the Bible, the reference to this meeting is intriguingly brief. The *Third Book of Kings* sketches the encounter in words beguiling enough to arouse our most blatant speculation.

> And the Queen of Sheba, having heard of the fame of Solomon, came to try him with hard questions, . . . and spoke to him all that she had in her heart.
> . . .
> And King Solomon gave the Queen of Sheba, all that she desired and asked of him, besides what he offered her of himself of his royal bounty. And she returned to her own country with her servants.

What were the questions? What heartfelt things did she tell him? What did he offer her? We can only guess at the answers. The hint of intimacy, however, is unmistakable.

Arabic tales tell us more about these royal lovers. Once again Solomon is the wise king. In the adventures told here he is further gifted with magical powers. Miraculously, he skims the world on a green silk flying carpet. Supposedly, on one of these trips, he first learned of the land of

Sheba and its lovely queen. When Sheba is mentioned in the Koran she is portrayed as a fabulous queen who married Solomon. In many of the Arabic tales told about them she emerges as a learned woman who tests Solomon with riddles, fencing with him in an intricate duel of wits. With each response he proves that his reputation for wisdom is justified.

The tale of these two lovers continues and is further embellished in the literature of the African country of Ethiopia. It is written in the thirteenth century Ethiopian epic, *Glory of Kings*, that there was a son, Menelek, from this royal encounter but that Solomon never knew of his existence. For some, belief in this kingly birth is so real that they still cling to the notion that the rightful rulers of Ethiopia are descendants of these stately lovers.

Solomon and Sheba came together in Israel's colorful capital city. By day they fulfilled their roles as King and Queen amongst the teeming populace. But by night, perhaps they sought the solitude of the cool quiet desert. With light hearts they might have retired to a luxurious tent under a star filled sky. With the whisper of a silken tent flap, the muted glow of oil lamps and the rustle of soft cushions, the public figures became the private man and woman.

Silent attendants placed an array of tempting dishes before their monarchs. Honey glazed game birds, flavorful barley pilaf, buttery turnip straws and the cool bite of a watercress salad were majestic offerings for a fabled King and Queen.

Watercress Salad

Since early man first discovered watercress growing wild it has been sought eagerly. Noted for its peppery taste, it is surprisingly refreshing. All the deep green leaves need is a simple dressing of good quality olive oil and lemon juice.

1   *small bunch watercress*
1   *tablespoon olive oil*
1   *teaspoon lemon juice*
pinch salt

Wash watercress thoroughly to remove all traces of sand. Shake to remove excess moisture. Cut off stems and any wilted leaves.

Mix olive oil, lemon juice, and salt in a small bowl. Toss lightly with cress just before serving.

Game Birds With Honey-Mustard Glaze

In ancient times, many foods uncommon by today's standards were available for daily consumption. Quail, partridge, and pheasant, the small game birds of antiquity, seem exotic to us. Consequently, catering to modern tastes, we have chosen the Cornish game hen, a readily available, specially bred bird, and an ideal substitute for these more unusual fowl.

Slow cooking and frequent basting produce a moist golden glazed entrée.

>   2   Cornish hens
>   ¼   cup honey
>   1½   teaspoons dry mustard
>   ¼   cup brandy
>   2   tablespoons butter
>   2   teaspoons parsley
>   ¼   teaspoon salt
>   dash pepper

Rinse birds and pat dry. Blend butter, parsley, salt, and pepper together. Divide mixture in half, placing each portion inside one of the birds. Tie the legs together with white kitchen cord. Bake for ½ hour in preheated 375°F. oven.

Meanwhile, prepare the brandy sauce for basting. In a small saucepan, over low heat, add mustard to brandy. Stir until thoroughly blended. Add honey and heat until the sauce is smooth. Set aside.

When birds have baked for ½ hour brush liberally with sauce. Return to oven and bake for another 45 minutes, brushing every 15 minutes. Remove from oven, clip cord, and serve.

Barley Pilaf

Barley, having been cultivated by early man even before wheat, is an appropriate accompaniment to our Biblical meal. Easily grown and versatile in nature it provides a pleasant nutty flavored side dish.

½   cup pearl barley, uncooked
3   tablespoons butter
1   small onion, minced
¼   cup mushrooms, sliced
1¾ cups chicken bouillion
pinch salt
dash pepper
1   tablespoon parsley
2   tablespoons pine nuts (optional)

Melt 1 tablespoon butter in a small frying pan. Add barley and sauté for 5 minutes. Transfer barley to a small heavy saucepan.

Melt 1 more tablespoon of butter in frying pan and sauté minced onion until it is translucent. Add to barley.

Sauté mushrooms in remaining tablespoons of butter and add these to the barley mixture.

Add hot bouillion, pine nuts, parsley, salt, and pepper to the barley mixture. Cook covered over very low heat until the barley is tender and has absorbed all the liquid. This will take 30 to 45 minutes. Stir occasionally.

Turnip Straws

Turnips have been grown for over 4000 years. Once considered a common vegetable suitable for the poor, turnips have risen above this early derision to become, for many, an admired vegetable fit for a gourmet's palate.

1   *small yellow turnip*
¼   *cup butter*
1   *teaspoon garlic salt*

Peel turnip and cut into thin strips. Parboil until cooked but still crunchy. Drain.
    Melt butter in a frying pan. Add cooked turnip straws and garlic salt. Toss lightly until the straws are well coated.

Walnut Fig Tart

Figs were synonymous with fruit in ancient times. There are numerous references to the fig in the Bible and they are said to have been grown in the Hanging Gardens of Babylon. Thousands of years ago inhabitants of Mesopotamia preserved figs by burying them in the hot desert sands. They also made them into a syrup, which was used as a sweetener.

We make use of figs which have been preserved in a more modern way as jam. Our tart is assembled in the same manner as a linzertorte, its lattice top offering a glimpse of the almost clear fig jam within.

    ¾   cup all-purpose flour
    5   tablespoons butter, softened
    ½   cup walnuts, ground
    1   tablespoon honey
    1   egg yolk
    1   10-ounce jar fig jam
    *confectioners' sugar

Preheat oven to 350°F. Blend flour, butter, walnuts, honey, and egg yolk together until they form a smooth ball. Set aside ⅓ of the dough for the lattice top. Spread the remaining dough over the bottom and 1 inch up the sides of a 8-inch spring form pan.

Spread the fig jam over the bottom of the tart shell. Using the remaining dough, make a lattice top, carefully sealing each strip to the bottom crust at the edges.

With the tines of a fork, gently press along the top of the crust all around the edge. This not only will seal the pieces, it will give the tart a more finished look.

Bake at 350°F. for 25 minutes. Cool completely before removing the side of the pan.

*Note: although confectioners' sugar was not present in the kitchen of antiquity, you may choose to sprinkle some on top of the finished tart.

ANTONY
AND
CLEOPATRA

Mark Antony, the Roman consul, demanded that Cleopatra come to him. When she did, he was as captivated as his predecessors, Pompey and Julius Caesar, had been. Before long, this beautiful and clever daughter of the pharaohs became his obsession. Seduced by her celebrated beauty, he abandoned family, duty, and friends, and dallied for years in Alexandria with the enchanting Queen of the Nile. So infatuated with her was he that he presented her with Roman provinces and kingdoms as tokens of his love.

When he became enamoured of Egypt's exotic queen, Mark Antony was a celebrated general and the acknowledged leader of half the Roman world. This brave soldier, who had been Caesar's friend and avenger, was at the height of his power.

Who was this woman who captured the hearts of three great Roman leaders? We are told that she was of Macedonian descent, probably blond, undeniably charming, and definitely shrewd. When she was summoned to Mark Antony, she set out to make herself irresistible to this noble son of Rome — and she succeeded.

Their love story began in Cilicia, a Roman province in the Middle East. Plutarch, that ancient biographer of famous Greeks and Romans, described Cleopatra's splendid arrival. He wrote that she came on a golden barge with perfumed sales and silver oars. Amid this luxury the Queen of Egypt reclined seductively under a gilded canopy, attended by nymph-like maidens clad in diaphanous gowns. Bedazzled, Mark Antony was powerless to resist her charms.

The consul and the queen reveled and feasted through endless days and nights of passion. Together they tried to win an empire by challenging

Octavius, Mark Antony's brother-in-law, for control of Rome. They failed. Following the defeat of their fleet at the battle of Actium in 31 B.C., the vanquished lovers fled back to Egypt. Octavius, pressing his advantage, followed with his army. With no hope of victory, a distraught Antony, following Roman tradition, fell upon his sword. Cleopatra, desiring to join her love, embraced the poisonous asp.

History has left us the story of these two lovers who defied all for love. But rather than dwell on their bitter end, let us remember instead their days of glorious passion. Imagine Cilicia's river bank bathed in moonlight. The alluring sound of flutes fills the air and Antony has accepted Cleopatra's invitation to dinner. Perhaps there were plates of beaten gold, goblets studded with jewels, and exotic foods from the far reaches of the empire. Caviar-stuffed eggs and feather-light fish fillets wrapped around sweet green grapes are served with broccoli from the Italian peninsula and small round yeast rolls. A multi-layered cream and apricot baklava completes this sumptuous meal. Throughout the meal wine flowed . . . and the world was theirs for the moment.

Caviar Stuffed Eggs

Sturgeon, the fish which provides caviar, was once prodigious in the Mediterranean, the North Sea, and the Atlantic Ocean. Today it is a victim of pollution and is lost to many of its former grounds. Most caviar is now imported from Russia although a small amount is gathered in other parts of the world.

Different sturgeon produce different types of caviar. The larger eggs are more expensive and usually have a lower salt content. We suggest using the most expensive caviar you can afford.

2	eggs
1	tablespoon caviar
2	teaspoons mayonnaise
½	teaspoon finely minced onion

Hard-cook the eggs and allow them to cool. Remove the shells and cut eggs in half lengthwise. Gently pry yolks out of egg halves. In a small bowl combine egg yolks, caviar, mayonnaise, and onion. Spoon ¼ of mixture back into each egg white. Chill until ready to serve. Before serving arrange egg halves on a bed of lettuce.

Dressing
2	tablespoons sour cream
2	teaspoons milk
1	tablespoon finely minced cucumber

Combine all ingredients and pour over stuffed eggs just before serving.

Baked Fish With Grapes

Among the Nile's many gifts to Egypt was its abundant aquatic life. Indeed eel, mullet, perch, and carp were staples of the Egyptian diet. These varieties of fish were enjoyed in many ways. This elegant fish fillet stuffed with grapes has a delicate flavor that is matched by a light wine sauce.

    1   *pound fillet of sole*
    2   *tablespoons butter*
    1   *tablespoon fresh red pepper, chopped*
    6   *medium mushrooms (with stems), chopped*
    1   *tablespoon minced shallot*
   ¼   *cup sliced green seedless grapes*
    1   *tablespoon chopped parsley*
   ⅛   *teaspoon salt*
   pinch white pepper
    1   *cup whole green grapes (for sauce)*

In a small pan melt butter. Sauté mushrooms, shallot, and parsley in butter until just softened. Add salt and pepper, mixing well. Remove mixture from heat. Stir in ¼ cup sliced grapes.

   Rinse fish and pat dry. Divide fillets into 4 pieces. Place equal amounts of filling in center of each piece. Roll and place (edges side down) in a shallow buttered 8-inch pan. Set aside while you prepare the sauce.

Wine Sauce

1 tablespoon butter
1 tablespoon all-purpose flour
½ cup heavy cream
¼ cup dry white wine
⅛ teaspoon salt
pinch cayenne pepper

In a small saucepan, melt butter and flour over medium heat. Stir with a wire whisk until all the flour has been incorporated into the butter. Add cream, wine, salt, and pepper, stirring constantly until the mixture is smooth.

Pour sauce over fish. This dish may be stored in the refrigerator until mealtime. To cook, bake at 375°F. for 15 minutes. Remove pan from oven and spoon some of the sauce over the fish. Add the 1 cup of whole grapes. Return to oven and bake for 10 minutes longer.

Broccoli

It may surprise you to learn that broccoli is part of the cabbage family. It was a favorite among the early Romans over 2000 years ago. To be sure that it retains its crispness, do not overcook it.

½   *pound fresh broccoli*
1 ½ *tablespoons butter*
½   *teaspoon lemon juice*
⅛   *teaspoon salt*
pinch pepper

Wash broccoli under cold water. Cut off the toughest part of the stem and leaves. Separate into flowerettes. Place broccoli in a covered saucepan in 1-inch of cold water. Bring to a boil. Lower heat to medium and cook for 5 to 10 minutes lifting the cover occasionally to keep the broccoli a dark green. Meanwhile, melt butter and combine with remaining ingredients. Drain broccoli and serve hot with lemon butter.

Water Rolls

Paintings on walls of Egyptian tombs illustrate the importance of bread in that culture. It was perhaps by chance that the ancient Egyptians discovered leavened bread. Imagine their delight at now having an alternative to the hard flat loaves of antiquity. Although the risen bread of 3000 B.C. was the sour dough variety, we make use of yeast here. By the time of Antony and Cleopatra it was in wide use.

½   cup warm water
1   teaspoon active dry yeast
1 ½ teaspoons sugar
1   teaspoon salt
1 ¾ cups sifted all-purpose flour
1   tablespoon olive oil
1   egg, separated (reserve yolk)
1 ½ teaspoon water

In a large bowl, combine water, sugar, salt, and yeast. Stir until the yeast is dissolved. Allow to proof for 5 minutes. Add ½ cup flour and the oil. Mix until the batter is smooth. Add egg white and remaining flour. Continue mixing until dough is relatively stiff.

Turn onto a floured board and knead lightly for about 5 minutes. If you are using an electric mixer, beat with dough hook for three minutes. Place dough in a greased bowl. Cover and let rise in a warm place until doubled in bulk. (Approximately 1 ½ hours.)

Punch down and turn onto a floured board. Allow to rest for 10 minutes. Cut dough into six pieces. Shape each piece into a ball and place on a greased baking sheet. Cover and let rise until doubled in bulk. (Approximately 45 minutes.)

Preheat oven to 400°F. Brush rolls with mixture of egg yolk and the 1 ½ teaspoon water. Bake for 15 to 20 minutes or until golden brown. Rolls may be frozen for future use.

Apricot Cream Baklava

Phyllo, tissue thin sheets of dough, is a versatile and popular type of pastry. Once only available in Middle Eastern kitchens, it now can be purchased in your local supermarket. Using this paper thin dough is not difficult as long as you remember to keep it covered and follow the directions on the package.

One of the ways to use phyllo is in a dessert called baklava. Traditionally this rich pastry contains layers of nuts and honey. Our version is somewhat different. Instead of nuts, we use apricot purée and a farina-based cream for the filling. The light layers of dough are barely discernible in this honey-glazed confection.

Apricot Filling
6   ounces dried apricots
⅔   cup sugar
¾   cup water

Soak apricots overnight in enough water to cover them. Discard this water before beginning to prepare filling.

Place apricots, ⅔ cup sugar, and ¾ cup water in a small saucepan. Cover and simmer for ½ hour over low heat. Remove from heat and cool slightly. Drain apricots, reserving liquid. Put apricots and 3 tablespoons of the cooking liquid in a blender. Purée until smooth. Reserve the rest of the cooking liquid for the glaze.

Cream Filling
1¾ cups milk
3   tablespoons sugar
¼   cup farina
⅛   teaspoon salt

Warm milk, sugar, and salt over medium heat. When mixture is steaming, add farina a little at a time, stirring constantly. Cook until pudding is thick and there are no lumps in it. When you are assembling the baklava, this mixture should be warm — for ease of spreading.

Assembly

30 sheets of phyllo dough 8" by 8"
½   cup sweet butter, melted

Follow directions on package of phyllo dough for thawing and handling. Butter the bottom of an 8-inch square baking pan. Place one sheet of phyllo on bottom. Brush sparingly with butter. Repeat until there are six layers.

Spread one half of the farina mixture over the pastry sheets. Cover with another six layers of buttered phyllo sheets. Then spread with ½ apricot purée. Repeat phyllo-filling assembly, ending with a layer of phyllo on the top. Brush top generously with melted butter. Before baking, cut into six portions with a sharp knife.

Bake in a preheated 350°F. oven for 35 to 40 minutes or until the top is light brown. Meanwhile, prepare the glaze.

Glaze

½   cup sugar
½   cup reserved liquid from apricots
¼   cup honey

Combine all ingredients in a small saucepan. Cook over medium heat until the sugar is dissolved. Allow to cool.

When baklava is golden brown, remove the pan from the oven and allow to sit for 15 minutes. Spoon the cooled syrup over the top slowly, allowing it to be gradually absorbed. Serve warm.

If baklava is made early in the day, reheat at 350°F. for 10 minutes before serving. Leftovers should be refrigerated. Reheat before serving again.

SCHEHERAZADE
AND
SULTAN SCHAHRIAR

Recorded by scribes in ancient Persia, India, and Arabia, and retold by poets in the Egyptian marketplace, the tale of the Sultan Schahriar and the Sultana Scheherazade is a love story like no other.

As early as the eighth century A.D., manuscripts have been found which relate this intriguing legend. Each version begins with the story of the Sultan of Baghdad, a man of wealth and power, who finds himself the victim of treachery at the hands of his first wife. As a result, he believes that all women are unfaithful and vows not to trust one again. Each evening for three years he desires a woman. But he takes a bride only to put her promptly to death the next morning. These acts enrage his people, who flee with their daughters until no girls of marriageable age remain.

The Sultan's trusted servant, the Wazir, agonizes for the maidens who meet with untimely death. Painfully he also bemoans his own fate at not being able to find any new wives for his master. At the point when he is fearful for his own life his daughter, Scheherazade, offers her own solution to his problem. In a desperate measure this beautiful and intelligent woman bids her father to offer her as a wife for the Sultan. The Wazir, knowing full well that should he do so it also would be his task to put his own daughter to death, withholds his consent. But Scheherazade assures him that this is his only choice and that, with luck, she will not meet with that horrible fate.

Her determination wins out and Scheherazade does indeed wed the Sultan. It is to be a night the Sultan will not forget. Wise as well as beautiful, the young maiden sets out to capture her husband's imagination. She begins to weave a fantasy composed of stories and poems which the Sultan finds irresistible. Cunningly, she ends the evening in the middle of her tale. In the morning the Sultan postpones her death for another day as he eagerly looks forward to the conclusion of her story. Legend tells us that after one thousand and one nights of these fantasies, the Sultan was so enamored and delighted by his wife that he gave up his bloody preoccupation and withdrew the threat of death from her.

It is no wonder that the tales of the Arabian nights have entertained people for centuries. Some of the most popular tales have become classics in the literary world. The best known of these are *The Story of Sinbad the Sailor, Aladdin and His Wonderful Lamp*, and *Ali Baba and the Forty Thieves*.

The world of music also pays tribute to this timeless love story. Most notable is the colorfully orchestrated *Schcherazade* by Rimsky-Korsakov. First performed in 1888, its theme was inspired by some of the composer's favorite fables and certainly evokes a fairy-tale quality for the listener.

The dreamy mood of Rimsky-Korsakov's music inspires us to imagine how Scheherazade and Schahriar might have lived. The wealthy Sultan certainly would have had a palace richly decorated with gold, silks, and jewel-toned oriental carpets. Each evening, sweet smelling perfumes would fill the air as the Sultan reclined on his raised couch. Seated before him the Sultana spun her tales, while feeding her husband tempting morsels of specially prepared food. From a hammered brass tray she may have chosen tissue thin sheets of phyllo dough filled with cooked lamb, chick pea croquettes, stuffed baby eggplant, and honey sweetened date cookies. You can entice your love with this Arabian assortment.

Crab and Feta Triangles

These small crisp triangles combine the mild taste of crab meat with the pungent flavor of feta cheese. The result is a filling with a marvelous tang surrounded by a buttery shell.

8	sheets of phyllo dough, 3" by 12"
¾	cup crab meat
¼	cup feta cheese
1	tablespoon minced scallions
½	teaspoon lemon juice
¼	teaspoon dried dill
1	teaspoon chopped parsley

pinch pepper

3	tablespoons butter

Handle phyllo dough according to the instructions on the package. Pick over crab meat for traces of shell. Rinse with cold water and drain. Combine crab meat, feta cheese, scallions, lemon juice, dill, parlsey, and pepper in a small bowl.

Melt butter over low heat. Brush single 3"x12" sheet of phyllo sparingly with butter. Fold in half so that the piece measures 3" by 6". Butter again. Place 1 teaspoon of filling in lower center. Fold right hand corner to meet left side forming a triangle. Continue to fold in this manner until entire sheet has been used. Place triangle on a cookie sheet and brush liberally with butter. Repeat until all of the mixture has been used.

Bake in preheated 350°F. oven for 10 minutes or until triangles are a golden brown. Serve hot.

Lamb Rolls

Today lamb is still the dominant meat in the Middle East. In Iraq evidence of domesticated sheep has been found dating back to 9000 B.C.. The taste of lamb is not the same everywhere nor is the definition of just when an animal is considered ideal for consumption. Regardless, visitors and natives agree that lamb raised in the Middle East is equal to or better than that found anywhere.

The lamb in this dish is cooked through in the Middle Eastern tradition. Mixed with vegetables and baked in a phyllo shell this dish has an especially delicate character.

1	pound ground lamb
2	tablespoons chopped scallions
1	small eggplant
⅓	cup chopped fresh red pepper
1	tablespoon butter
¼	teaspoon thyme
1	tablespoon chopped parsley
2	tablespoons lemon juice
¼	teaspoon salt
⅛	teaspoon pepper
16	strips of phyllo dough cut 6" by 12"
⅓	cup melted butter

Peel eggplant and cut into ½-inch chunks. Measure 1 cup and combine with red pepper. Set aside.

Crumble lamb into a medium-size frying pan and brown over medium heat. When meat has lost its pink color, drain fat and put lamb aside in a bowl.

In the same pan, melt butter over low heat. Add scallions, eggplant, and red pepper and cook for about five minutes until vegetables are soft. Add spices, lemon juice, and browned meat. Cook for 2 to 3 minutes. Remove from heat.

Follow instructions on package for handling phyllo dough. To assemble, brush one side of phyllo dough sparingly with melted butter. Fold in half so that dimensions are now 6" by 6". Brush again with butter. Place 1 tablespoon of meat mixture in center lower area of square. Fold outer edges to center and roll securely from bottom up. Place edge side down on a greased baking sheet and brush generously with butter. Bake in preheated 350°F. oven for 15 minutes.

Lamb rolls may be frozen. You do not need to defrost before baking.

Chick Pea Croquettes

Chick peas have been grown for so long that it is impossible to accurately pin-point the time they were first eaten. Evidence of their existence has been found in Neolithic and prehistoric ruins. They are grown extensively in the Middle East, Africa and many poorer countries where they are an important factor in staving off famine. These croquettes have a crunchy outer shell and are flavored with subtle spices from the Middle East.

1   cup canned chick peas
1   egg
2½ tablespoons cracked wheat
¼   teaspoon coriander
1   tablespoon parsley
⅛   teaspoon turmeric
½   teaspoon cumin
½   clove garlic
½   small onion, minced
2   tablespoons all-purpose flour
½   teaspoon salt
⅛   teaspoon cayenne pepper
lemon wedges
vegetable oil

Place cracked wheat in a bowl and cover with water. Allow to soak for 2 hours. In a blender or food processor, purée chick peas, cracked wheat, spices, onion, garlic, and flour until smooth. Allow to sit for 15 minutes before proceeding.

Heat ½-inch oil in frying pan. When oil is very hot drop chick pea mixture by teaspoonsful into oil leaving a space between each croquette. Brown thoroughly on each side and drain on paper towels. Keep those that are finished in a warm oven while cooking the remaining croquettes. Sprinkle with lemon juice and serve.

You can prepare the croquettes early in the day and reheat them just before serving. Don't sprinkle with the lemon juice until serving time.

Stuffed Baby Eggplant

It is said that eggplant has been eaten for 4,000 years. In the Arab world it plays an important part in the diet. Stuffed and baked is but one of the many ways it can be cooked.

    3   baby eggplants (about 2" long)
    1   tablespoon chopped onion
    1   tablespoon tomato paste
    ½   clove garlic, minced
    1   teaspoon chopped parsley
    2   tablespoons bread crumbs
    ⅛   teaspoon salt
    pinch pepper
    2   teaspoons lemon juice
    ½   teaspoon sugar
    3   tablespoons olive oil

Cut eggplants in half lengthwise and hollow out with a grapefruit knife. Leave a shell thick enough to stuff. Sauté halves quickly in 1 tablespoon olive oil. Transfer, skin side down, to a greased baking pan.

Chop pulp and sauté in 2 tablespoons olive oil. Add onion and garlic and continue cooking until onion is soft. Add parsley, salt, pepper, bread crumbs, lemon juice, and sugar. Cook for 2 to 3 minutes.

Brush insides of eggplant shells with olive oil. Fill each with ⅙ of mixture. Brush tops with olive oil and bake in preheated 350°F. oven for 20 minutes.

Honey Date Cookies

The Greeks thought dates a symbol of fertility and riches. Long prized by man, the date palm has been cultivated for thousands of years for its fruit, leaves, and fiber.

In the ancient world dates had a universal appeal. They were eaten as a fruit, fermented into wine, and cooked into a sweet syrup. Although dates can be eaten fresh they must be dried before shipping and this is how they appear in today's markets.

Like the date, honey is also one of man's earliest foods. It remained the principal sweetener until replaced by sugar some time after the thirteenth century A.D.

Dough
4   tablespoons butter
1   cup sifted all-purpose flour
¼   cup sour cream

In an electric mixer or food processor blend all ingredients until they form a smooth ball. Set aside.

Filling
½   cup (4 ounces) dates, chopped
¼   cup (2 ounces) walnuts, ground
1   medium apple, chopped
2   tablespoons honey
2   tablespoons milk
¼   teaspoon ground cinnamon
2   tablespoons slivered almonds (for garnish)

In a small bowl, mix all ingredients except milk together. The honey will hold the mixture together and make it slightly sticky.

On a floured pastry board, roll dough to ⅛" thickness. Cut into 3" circles. Place 1 teaspoon filling in center of each circle. Fold over into half-moon and seal edges with a fork. Brush with milk.

Bake in preheated 425°F. oven on center rack for 10 minutes or until cookies are golden brown. Remove from oven and place on wire cooling rack. While still hot brush with honey and sprinkle with slivers of almond.

DERMATT
AND
GRANIA

The Irish saga of Dermatt and Grania is a romantic story filled with sudden love, jealousy, and revenge. This Celtic tale tells of the beautiful Princess Grania, daughter of the King of Tara. She has been espoused to the elderly Finn of Fena, a fierce military leader. At their betrothal banquet the lovely maiden spies the handsome young warrior, Dermatt O'Dyna. Forsaking her intended, she vows to be his, whatever the cost.

The brave hero is fully aware of the dire consequences of succumbing to this sudden passion but, under the influence of Grania's Druid trickery, he agrees to flee with her. They run for their lives and traverse the length and breadth of Erin to escape the jealous wrath of the vengeful Finn. From Athlone to Killarney, to Limerick and Kerry and onward to Slige, the two lovers trek, sleeping on boughs under the stars.

As their flight continues, Dermatt faces many adventures and countless challenges to keep his wife beside him. With his spears, Ga-derg (the great red one), and Ga-boi (the small yellow one), and his swords Moralta (great fury), and Begalta (little fury), he faces life and death struggles in the name of love. Dermatt withstands attack after attack by valiant champions committed to his destruction. He battles venomous hounds, a one-eyed surly giant, magic spells, and the unceasing bitter anger of the leader of the Fena. It is only when Finn's own brave sons refuse to continue the feud and threaten to support Dermatt that the rejected suitor finally agrees to abandon his pursuit of the lovers. Dermatt and Grania find peace at last from their trials and dwell for years at Rath-Grania, their secluded country home.

During their travels, these Gaelic lovers ate from the riches of the forest: boar roasted over a great fire, salmon caught with a spear, and water from the clear springs of the Emerald Isle. Our contemporary choices make shopping for this romantic dinner easier. Nonetheless, the ingredients are sufficiently Irish to conjure up visions of these long-ago lovers from Irish mythology and their desparate flight to happiness.

To begin a dinner "in the Irish manner" might we raise a glass of dark, frothy Guinness stout and offer an old Gaelic toast to Dermatt and Grania? "Bean ar do mhian agat" — The woman of your choice to you. Then sample some tiny slivers of incomparable smoked Irish salmon served with slices of ripe melon. The Limerick ham, colcannon, and soda bread that follow are all highlights of the wholesome cuisine of Erin.

Smoked Salmon with Melon

Salmon has long been a favorite of royalty. This magnificent fish often appeared on the banquet tables of the ancient kings of Ireland. Today Irish smoked salmon still is among the best in the world. Served in paper thin slices, with a wedge of chilled ripe melon, it is a royal beginning to this gaelic dinner.

2   *ounces thin sliced smoked salmon*
2   *2" wedges of honeydew, cantalope, or cranshaw melon*

Limerick Ham Steak

The flavor of ham varies according to the breed of hog, the food it is fed, and the manner in which the ham is cured. The Irish have their own special way of preparing ham. A true Limerick ham is soaked and boiled and then perhaps baked before it is served. Fortunately, most American hams do not require all these steps. This recipe allows you to sample an Irish favorite without having to visit Ireland. The crunchy honey glaze sweetens the ham and seals in its juices while baking.

1   *1 pound boneless ham steak, about ¾" thick*
2   *tablespoons cream sherry*
2   *tablespoons honey*
4   *tablespoons bread crumbs*

Mix sherry, honey, and bread crumbs. Pour over ham steak and bake in preheated 375°F. oven for 30 minutes.

Colcannon

Although it is not a native to Ireland, the potato has long been a part of the Irish diet. It appears as though potatoes are only native to the high peaks of the Andes Mountains in South America. They are thought to have been cultivated several thousand years ago. In the years since their gradual spread to other South American countries and the rest of the world, they have become one of man's most important foodstuffs.

Cabbage is one of the oldest cultivated vegetables and can be prepared in many ways. It has long been a dependable food source for the people of Ireland. This dish combines these two staples of the Irish garden.

2	medium potatoes
1	cup finely chopped cabbage
1	tablespoon minced onion
¼	teaspoon salt
⅛	teaspoon pepper
2	tablespoons butter
¼	cup light cream

Peel and boil potatoes until tender. Mash well. In bowl of an electric mixer beat potatoes, light cream, butter, salt, and pepper until fluffy.

Meanwhile cook cabbage and onion in ½ cup water for 10 minutes. Drain. Fold cabbage into potatoes. Spoon into a buttered casserole, dot with butter, and warm in preheated 325°F. oven before serving.

Irish Soda Bread

Ask three Irish women for a recipe for soda bread and you'll get three different versions of what you will be told is the authentic Irish bread. One will add caraway seeds and raisins, another will swear that only a plain bread is genuine. However, they all will agree on most of the other ingredients. For decades this round loaf of soda bread was baked on a griddle before a turf fire. Today it is easily made in an oven in your kitchen. Buttermilk, the liquid that is left after butter is churned, gives this solid bread its unique texture and flavor. Whether or not you add the seeds and raisins be sure to cut a cross in the top before baking. This is done not necessarily to bless the bread but to avoid a sticky middle when the bread has finished baking.

    2   cups sifted all-purpose flour
    ½   cup sugar
    ½   teaspoon baking soda
    ½   teaspoon salt
    1   tablespoon caraway seeds
    ½   cup raisins
    1 ¼ cups buttermilk

Plump raisins by soaking them in hot water for 10 minutes. Sift dry ingredients. Add drained raisins and toss. Gradually add buttermilk and beat at medium speed of electric mixer until dough is moist but not sticky. Turn onto a floured board and knead for 2 minutes. Shape into a round loaf and place on greased 8-inch round pan or 9x5-inch loaf pan. Cut cross into the top with a sharp knife. Bake on center rack in preheated 350°F. oven for 40 minutes or until done. Test for doneness; loaf will sound hollow when you tap the bottom with your knuckles.

Irish Coffee

The delight of this after dinner concoction is the contrast between the hot, whiskey-flavored coffee and the cool sweetened whipped cream that graces the top. Be sure to use freshly brewed strong coffee for the best results. Serving this fancy coffee in a traditional Irish coffee goblet will give you a chance to appreciate it with your eyes as well as your taste buds.

    1   ounce Irish whiskey
    1   teaspoon sugar
    hot strong coffee
    ¼   cup heavy cream
    2   tablespoons sugar

Beat heavy cream and 2 tablespoons sugar until it forms stiff peaks. Pour whiskey into bottom of cup or Irish coffee goblet. Add 1 teaspoon sugar. Fill with coffee to within ½″ of top. Cover with chilled whipped cream.

84   PEALE.

LANCELOT AND GUINEVERE

Arthurian legend is a richly embroidered tapestry of marvelous adventure, glorious quests, and elegant courtly ritual. Among the many tales told of King Arthur and his knights of the Round Table, none is more human than the love story of Lancelot and Guinevere. Caught between their loyalty to Arthur and their desire for each other, these great lovers were destined to destroy the fabled kingdom of Camelot.

Their love may have begun innocently enough. In fact, the rules of courtly love encouraged an elaborate display of devotion between a gentle knight and his fair lady. Sir Lancelot du lac, the most handsome and valiant of Sir Arthur's knights, was sworn to protect the beautiful English queen. In this role, according to the code of medieval chivalry, the handsome warrior would exchange tokens with her. He might wear a silk scarf or another symbol of the lady's regard in contests of valor. She, in turn, as the object of his adoration, was supposed to be cool and distant.

The boundaries of this stylized love were firmly fixed. When somehow admiration turned to desire, the lovers stepped into the realm of the forbidden. Arthur's friend, the knight he loved and honored most, betrayed him by falling in love with the queen.

We will never know why the loyal knight and the virtuous queen fell from grace. Perhaps Arthur was too good, too caught up in his vision of a new world based on the principles of the Round Table. Maybe destiny played a role in their sinful love. Merlin, his advisor, had warned Arthur that Guinevere would someday deceive him. Whatever the reason, Lancelot and Guinevere were powerless to resist each other.

Time passes . . . The court is rife with rumors of their love. Guinevere has seen vague suspicion in Arthur's eyes. The threat of discovery adds an urgency to their meeting and in spite of the danger the secret lovers chance an evening alone, far from the prying eyes of the scandal-loving courtiers.

On a blustery winter evening, sheltered within the thick-walled castle, Lancelot and Guinevere recline before a blazing fire in the queen's apartments. They sip a heady mulled wine, lost in dreams of each other. For dinner they sup on a succulent roast pork flavored with thyme, a golden baked onion pudding, and lightly puffed fritters made from autumn's russet-skinned apples. As the evening ends they share a plum covered almond cream and savor their few stolen moments together.

Mulled Wine

Wine and ale were very much appreciated on the English table. Since most of the wine in the Middle Ages was homemade, spices were often added to improve the flavor.

1   *bottle Burgundy wine*
2   *2" cinnamon sticks*
½   *lemon, sliced thin*
2   *whole cloves*
¼   *cup sugar*
pinch nutmeg

Combine all ingredients in a saucepan. Heat well but do not boil. Strain and serve.

Pork Roast With Thyme

Probably the descendents of the wild boar, pigs have been domesticated since around 5,000 B.C. in both Egypt and China. During the Middle Ages the chief fresh meat of the upper classes was game. These people also dined on suckling pig. In the fall others, less well-to-do, also ate fresh pork — available because the farmers slaughtered their pigs rather than feed them through the long cold winter months.

> 2 to 2½ pounds boneless pork loin, rolled and tied
> 1   clove garlic
> ½   teaspoon thyme
> ⅛   teaspoon salt
> dash pepper
> 1   tablespoon butter
> ½   cup dry red wine

Preheat oven to 350°F. Place pork roast in a shallow roasting pan. Cut garlic clove in half and rub meat thoroughly on all sides. Discard garlic halves.

Combine thyme, salt and pepper and pat over surface of meat. Bake for 40 minutes per pound or until an oven thermometer reads 180°. Remove roast to a warm platter.

Pour off fat from roasting pan. Set pan on top of stove over a medium heat. Add ½ cup wine. With a spoon gently loosten the drippings from the bottom of the pan. Then add the butter. Stir liquid and heat gently until butter is melted and mixture simmers. Pour into gravy bowl and serve with sliced pork.

Broad Beans

Broad beans are similar to green beans except they are wider and have a slightly thicker skin. You will sometimes see them labeled as Italian green beans. Use fresh beans for best flavor and color.

½   *pound broad beans*
water
1   *tablespoon butter*

Wash beans under cold water. Trim ends and any dark spots. Cut into 1″ diagonal slices. Bring 1 inch of water to boil in a small saucepan. Add beans and cook uncovered for 10 minutes. Beans should be bright green and still crunchy. Drain. Toss with butter and serve.

Onion Pudding

In Medieval cookery puddings were a standard offering. These thick milk based casseroles were sometimes flavored with vegetables or fruit. The onion was grown in gardens on the feudal estates. Its popularity as a vegetable made it a natural ingredient for puddings.

> 1   cup sliced onions
> ¼   teaspoon sage
> 2   tablespoons butter
> 2   tablespoons water
> 1   tablespoon all-purpose flour
> ½   cup light cream
> ¼   cup bread crumbs
> 1   egg, beaten
> ½   teaspoon salt
> large pinch black pepper

Preheat oven to 350°F. Butter a 7½-inch loaf pan. Melt 1 tablespoon butter in a small saucepan. Add onions, sage, and water. Cook over low heat until onions are very limp and pale yellow. Set aside.

In a separate pan melt the remaining tablespoon of butter and add flour. Stir with a whisk until butter is incorporated into flour. Add cream and cook, stirring constantly, until mixture thickens to make a thin white sauce. Cool for 5 minutes. Transfer to medium-size bowl. Then gradually add beaten egg. Keep stirring to prevent egg from scrambling. Then add onions, bread crumbs, salt, and pepper. Mix thoroughly. Pour into buttered loaf pan and bake for 30 to 35 minutes until custard sets.

Apple Fritters

Fritters were a very popular side dish in the Middle Ages. These fritters are characteristically crisp on the outside and moist on the inside. For best results they should be cooked quickly in very hot oil.

2	medium Cortland apples
½	cup sifted all-purpose flour
½	teaspoon baking powder
1	tablespoon sugar
1	tablespoon brandy
¼	cup milk
½	teaspoon vanilla extract
pinch salt	
¼	cup sugar + 1 teaspoon ground cinnamon for topping

Peel and core apples. Cut into ¼" slices. In a small bowl combine all ingredients (except topping) and stir until just blended. Heat oil over medium-high heat until a drop of water skitters across the top. Dip apple slices into batter and place in hot oil leaving a space between each one. As you work keep finished fritters warm until others are ready. Dust with cinnamon and sugar. Serve immediately.

Almond Cream with Plum Sauce

This dessert is reminiscent of a blanc mange, an almond milk pudding that was often served during the Middle Ages. This is a modern method of preparation. When you unmold the white cream and decorate it with the plum sauce, we know you will be delighted with the way it looks and tastes.

    1½ teaspoons unflavored gelatin
    2   tablespoons cold water
    2   egg yolks
    ⅓   cup granulated sugar
    1¼ cups milk, scalded
    ½   teaspoon almond extract
    dash salt
    ½   cup heavy cream, whipped

In a small dish soak gelatin in water. Set aside.

Beat egg yolks with sugar until thick and lemon colored. Slowly stir in hot milk. Return mixture to saucepan or top of double boilder. Cook over medium-low heat until sauce thickens and bubbles. Do not over cook. Add gelatin and stir until smooth. Remove from heat and cool.

When mixture is cool fold in whipped cream and almond extract until sauce is smooth and well blended. Pour into a lightly greased (use vegetable oil) 2-cup mold. Refrigerate until firm. Before serving unmold onto plate and spoon on plum sauce.

Plum Sauce

½   cup cooked plums, puréed
⅓   cup damson plum preserves
1   teaspoon cornstarch

Combine cornstarch and jam in small saucepan. Add puréed plums and cook over low heat until sauce is thick and satiny. Stir constantly. Cool before serving.

ROMEO AND JULIET

Almost as soon as the word "Lovers" comes to mind, perhaps the next thought to follow is of the most famous pair of lovers of all time: Romeo and Juliet. Those two names immediately evoke the tragically poignant tale of the young "star-crossed" lovers caught in the web of their parents' ancient feud. That brief, beautiful love story spans centuries and still has the power to touch our hearts today as it has touched others for centuries.

For most of us, our knowledge of these fated Capulets and Montagues comes principally from Shakespeare's play, which appeared at the end of the sixteenth century. But the story of Romeo and Juliet apparently was well-known even before Shakespeare's version, having been told earlier in Italian, French — even English.

Probably Shakespeare's immediate source was the English poem by Arthur Brooke entitled *The Tragicall History of Romeus and Juliet*, which was printed in 1562. The interesting thing about Brooke's poem is that it covers a longer period of time than Shakespeare's play. The inevitably doomed lovers have nine secret months together before their suicides. In the play they have only five days of blinding love, fraught with danger, heartache, and finally death. Their grand passion flares from love at first sight to the blazing crescendo of their one night alone. They are always aware of the terrible danger they face, but, in spite of this, they choose to love each other. The famous balcony scene is clear evidence of their mutual adoration. And yet, it is all so beautiful, so brief, and so sad.

The love story of Romeo and Juliet will never fade. Whether you would like to believe that they had nine clandestine months together or one desperate night . . . so sweet, so poignant that it almost held back the dawn. Imagine if you will that Juliet's faithful nurse — the only one privy to their stolen moment — has arranged for a tray laden with a cold supper for the lovers to share. They begin with a rich cheese custard pie, or Torta, made from Italian cheeses and flavored with prosciutto. The second course, an aromatic salmon, is poached in a court bouillon laden with wine and herbs. It is served chilled, accompanied by a selection of crudités (favored by Italian cooks of the sixteenth century), and a pasta salad. A fitting end for this light supper is small almond butter cookies topped with quince jelly. Most likely they would have chosen a white wine from the Verona vineyards; a variety you might find on a wine shelf today.

Torta di Formaggio

This is a delightful combination of eggs and cheese spiced with a smoky Italian ham. Formerly a specialty of Italy, this highly prized ham is now widely available. You can prepare this dish early in the day and serve at room temperature.

2	ounces prosciutto, shredded
4	ounces fontina cheese, cubed
¼	cup Parmesan cheese, grated
3	eggs
1	cup light cream
⅛	teaspoon white pepper
1	teaspoon parsley, crushed
1	9" plain pie crust

Prepare a plain single pie crust. Bake in preheated 450°F. oven for 5 minutes. Remove from oven.

Cover bottom of pie shell with shredded prosciutto and cubed fontina cheese. Beat eggs, cream and white pepper together. Pour over other ingredients.

Sprinkle top with Parmesan cheese and parsley. Bake at 450°F. for 10 minutes. Reduce oven temperature to 350°F. and bake for 20 to 25 minutes more.

Poached Salmon with Dill Sauce

Salmon has long been high on the list of favorite fish consumed around the world. The simple elegance of poached salmon is one of the main reasons for its universal appeal. The pink meat, moist and delicately seasoned, is delicious whether served hot or cold. We suggest preparing the salmon early in the day. Wrapping it in cheesecloth while cooking will make it easier to handle but is not an absolute necessity. The garniture suggested is one which would have been available in the sixteenth century kitchen. You may add others if you like.

1½	pounds fresh salmon	**Crudités:**
1	cup dry white wine	sliced lemon
½	teaspoon salt	olives
1	carrot	parsley
1	stalk celery	onions
1	small onion	capers
2	peppercorns	lettuce
1	bay leaf	
½	teaspoon tarragon	
⅛	teaspoon thyme	
1	sprig fresh parsley	

In a medium saucepan combine all ingredients (except crudités) and bring to a boil. Lower heat and simmer for 10 minutes.

Place fish carefully in liquid. Cover and cook for 10 minutes on each side. Remove fish to a plate and cool. When cooled carefully peel off skin. Cover and refrigerate until serving time.

Just before serving arrange on a platter and decorate with vegetable garniture and lemon.

Dill Sauce

Most probably the sixteenth century kitchen did not have access to mayonnaise but fortunately we do. We think this cold sauce is a perfect accent for the "King of Fish."

¼   cup mayonnaise
¼   cup sour cream
1   tablespoon chopped fresh dill

Combine all ingredients and mix well. Chill until serving time.

Orzo Salad

It is an historical anecdote that pasta was first brought to Italy from China by Marco Polo. Today there are more than one hundred varieties of pasta. Depending on its use, it takes on many different shapes and sizes. For this dinner we chose orzo, a rice shaped pasta, which is often used in soups or rice pilaf. By flavoring the orzo while it is hot the pasta is better able to absorb the vinegar and oil.

1   cup orzo, uncooked
2   tablespoons olive oil
1   tablespoon wine vinegar
1   tablespoon green onion, minced
¼   teaspoon salt
pinch pepper

Cook orzo in one quart of boiling water for 15 minutes. Drain. While pasta is still hot, stir in the remaining ingredients. Refrigerate until serving time. For best results use a good quality olive oil.

Amoretti

The name for these delightfully rich small cookies is actually a small play on words. Amaretti is the familiar name for Italian almond macaroons. *Amoretti* is the title of Edmund Spenser's sequence of love sonnets written in the sixteenth century meaning "little love poems" or "Cupid's bows." Hence our "Amoretti" for Romeo and Juliet and you.

Two of the ingredients used in these "love cookies" are almonds and quince, staples of the Italian Renaissance kitchen. The piquant flavor of the rather tart quince jelly is the perfect foil for the buttery almond dough. Quince, in particular, is an appropriate ingredient as it was considered sacred to the Goddess of Love by the Greeks and Romans.

6	tablespoons butter
¼	cup light brown sugar, firmly packed
1	cup sifted all-purpose flour
½	teaspoon almond extract
¼	cup blanched almonds, finely ground
¼	teaspoon ground cinnamon
1½	teaspoons granulated sugar
¼	cup quince jelly (If you cannot find quince jelly a good quality apple jelly may be substituted.)
16	slivered almonds

With a pastry blender combine butter, brown sugar, flour, almond extract, and ground nuts until some of the dough squeezed in your hands holds together. Pat dough into an ungreased 8-inch square pan and prick entire surface with a fork. Mix cinnamon and granulated sugar together and sprinkle on top of dough.

Arrange 16 ½-teaspoons of jelly on the top dividing the dough evenly. Place a slivered almond on top of each dab of jelly.

Bake in preheated 325°F. oven for 15 minutes or until the top is a light brown. Cool in pan for 15 minutes. Then cut into 16 small rectangles. Remove from pan and cool completely on a rack.

SHAH JAHAN AND MUMTAZ MAHAL

Legend tells us that in 1607, amid the gaily colored tents of the Royal Meena Bazaar in Agra, India, Prince Khurram, son of the Mogul emperor, Jahangir, fell in love at first sight with Arjumand Banu Begam, daughter of the prime minister. Defying tradition, the young prince asked his father for permission to marry the beautiful noblewoman, mindful of the fact that marrying for love was unheard of in India at that time. The emperor, who had himself succumbed to the love of one woman, granted his son's wish.

Still, it took five years for the lovers to be united. During that time they were not allowed even the briefest meeting. Finally on March 27, 1612 the two were married. The emperor, an admirer of his son's wife, bestowed upon her the high honor of a new name, one which announced her elevated status to all. The young woman became known as Mumtaz Mahal, "Chosen One of the Palace."

Eventually Khurram took over his father's throne and together the new Shah Jahan and his beautiful wife reigned over the nation. In the nineteen years they were together Mumtaz Mahal bore fourteen children. It was during the birth of their fourteenth child that the queen died.

The legend continues. It is said that after the death of his beloved, the Shah went into seclusion for eight days. On the ninth day he emerged, physically and emotionally changed forever. The formerly handsome, straight backed, worldly Shah was now a white haired, stooped old man. His resplendent robes were permanently exchanged for the simple white Moslem robes of mourning. During his almost two years of mourning the Shan devised a plan for a spectacular mausoleum for his queen. In its grandeur the Taj Mahal remains the most glorious testimonial to a woman ever built.

It is impossible to describe in a few words the complex arrangement of rooms, courtyards, and hallways that make up the Taj Mahal. Elegant white marble walls and towers inlaid with precious gems, lush well planned gardens, and a reflecting pool are the ingredients; together they form a mystical illusion that must be viewed in person to be fully understood. Visitors say that the spirit of the love between Shah Jahan and Mumtaz Mahal still can be felt there today.

This much loved woman held a unique place in her husband's life as his lover, confidant, and trusted adviser. It was not uncommon for the Shah to visit with her in the evening to relax and share the burdens of ruling an empire. In her magnificent suite of rooms, laden with the opulent treasures of the Moguls, Mumtaz Mahal prepares for the arrival of her husband. From the courtyard below the muted splash of a fountain filters through diaphanous curtains billowing gently in the breeze. The scent of Indian spices fills the room as dinner warms on a low brazier. Although bound by Moslem tradition, these Indian lovers still are able to enjoy some of the most popular dishes in Northern India.

Succulent lamb marinated in yoghurt and spiced with curry, a flavorful rice pilaf studded with raisins and nuts, and whole wheat chapati form the basis of their meal. These classics are followed by fresh fruit with gingered yoghurt dressing, soft music, and whispered conversation.

Pistachio Fried Eggplant

This dish combines two ingredients which are very popular in Indian cooking. Nuts are very often added to a variety of dishes while eggplant is pleasantly prepared in many ways. We suggest that this dish be served immediately after cooking so that the eggplant retains its moist consistency and the nuts are still crunchy. Serve these golden patties with your favorite brand of fruit chutney.

1   *small eggplant*
1   *cup pistachio nuts, shelled and finely ground*
¼   *cup all-purpose flour*
1   *egg beaten with 1 tablespoon water*
4   *tablespoons butter*

Peel eggplant and cut into ¼″ slices. Dip eggplant into flour, egg, and then ground pistachio nuts. Coat evenly.

In a frying pan over medium heat, melt butter. Sauté eggplant on both sides until it is a golden brown.

Curried Lamb

Indian food is characterized by generous use of spices. Before beginning to use them in your cooking we suggest a visit to a Middle Eastern gourmet shop. There spices and other distinctive ingredients are sold in single quantities and you will be able to gain an appreciation for the different components of your Indian meal.

For our spicy lamb we experimented with fresh store bought curry powder and our own combination of spices. We found the pre-measured powder very satisfying mainly because it enhanced rather than masked the natural flavor of the lamb. If you like the lamb made with curry powder you might be encouraged to experiment on your own. There are easy ways to make this dish hotter if you so desire. If you should make the mistake of getting it too hot, rest assured, eventually the fire in your mouth will go out.

2	pounds lamb, carefully trimmed and cubed
1	cup plain yogurt
2	teaspoons fresh curry powder
1½	teaspoons lemon juice
⅛	teaspoon nutmeg
⅛	teaspoon mace
⅛	teaspoon ground cinnamon
⅛	teaspoon freshly ground pepper
1	teaspoon salt
2	tablespoons butter
2	large yellow onions, chopped
2	cloves garlic, minced
	pinch sugar
1	teaspoon ginger root, finely chopped

In a medium bowl combine lamb, yoghurt, lemon juice, and spices. Prepare early in the day and refrigerate or marinate for two hours at room temperature.

Cook in a medium-sized saucepan. Brown onions and garlic in butter. Add rest of ingredients. Stir well. Cover and simmer over low heat for one hour.

Rice Pilaf

The addition of fruit and nuts to rice makes it a very rich side dish. A traditional Indian pilaf or "biryani" would be even richer than this recipe. At one time serving of this dish announced to all the wealth of the host.

½   cup uncooked white rice
1 ½ cups chicken bouillon
1   tablespoon onion, chopped
2   tablespoons butter
⅛   teaspoon ground cinnamon
¼   cup dark raisins
2   tablespoons roasted cashews

In a small saucepan sauté the chopped onion in butter until it is soft. Add the rice and cook for 1 to 2 minutes. Add the bouillion, cinnamon, and raisins. Cover and lower heat. Cook until all the liquid is absorbed.

Just before serving add cashews and stir rice with a fork.

Chapati

Chapati were traditionally the "poor man's" bread in India. Today they are enjoyed by everyone regardless of social class. There are several ways to prepare them. Sometimes oil is included in the recipe or there is a mixture of white and whole-wheat flours. We favor a whole-wheat flour recipe which will prove to be a delightful authentic addition to your meal.

While chapati are not difficult to make you must give them your undivided attention during preparation — especially while the pancakes are under the broiler. Served warm with butter these crisp puffs are well worth the effort.

>   1 ¼ cups whole-wheat flour
> ¼   teaspoon salt
> Approximately ½ cup cold water

Mix flour and salt. Stir in the water a little at a time. Mix until you have a firm dough. Knead for 2 to 3 minuts.

Break off a piece about the size of a quarter. Roll as thin as you can. Cook quickly on both sides on an ungreased griddle.

Turn on broiler. Place chapati in a single layer on a baking sheet. Place pan under broiler for 1 to 2 minutes. Watch carefully. Dough will puff up and brown slightly. Turn and brown on other side.

Mango with Yogurt Dressing

The mango has been known since history began. It is thought to have originated in Eastern India where not only is the fruit prized but its tree is considered sacred. Today India still produces most of the world's mangoes. This distinctive fruit has an unusual taste and texture. It is a refreshing companion to the spicy tang of the lamb curry.

1	large mango
4	ounce plain yogurt
1	tablespoon sugar
¼	teaspoon ground ginger

Peel mango and carefully cut it in sections. Arrange on two dessert plates. Combine yogurt, sugar and ginger in a small bowl. Allow to sit for 10 minutes. Spoon over mango and serve.

PRISCILLA
AND
JOHN ALDEN

Truth and legend are inextricably entwined in the love story of John Alden and Priscilla Mullens. History teaches us that these two pilgrims, who arrived in Plymouth on the Mayflower in 1620, were among the first settlers in America. Managing to survive famine, sickness, and the harsh New England weather, they married and lived a long and fruitful life. To this day their descendants gather regularly at the Alden House in Duxbury, Massachusetts, where John Alden was a founding father.

How then did a legend emerge immortalizing this famous pair? In essence, it grew out of an anecdote concerning their courtship and marriage, and was preserved by a nineteenth century American poet. Although it is a little known fact, Henry Wadsworth Longfellow was a direct descendant of John and Priscilla Alden. In 1856, interweaving fact and fantasy, he wrote the romantic poem, "The Courtship of Miles Standish."

In it we read of a sentimental if not passionate love triangle. John Alden is persuaded to woo Priscilla Mullens for his friend Miles Standish in spite of his own secret yearnings for her. To his amazement,

> . . . as he warmed and glowed, in his simple and eloquent language
> Quite forgetful of self, and full of the praise of his rival,
> Archly the maiden smiled, and, with eyes overrunning with laughter
> Said, in a tremulous voice, 'Why don't you speak for yourself, John?'

With those few words John rejoiced, knowing that the Puritan maiden returned his love. However, his overwhelming happiness turned immediately to bitter despair; torn between friendship and love, he realized there was no hope for them.

Months later, when Miles Standish is reported killed in a skirmish with the Indians, John and Priscilla decide to marry. During the wedding ceremony, a ghostly apparition appears, seemingly to challenge the union. However it proves to be a very alive Captain Standish come to offer his blessings to the happy couple. The romantic poem concludes as the bridal procession meanders through a pastoral forest to their new home where love "Old and yet ever new, and simple and beautiful always . . ." will flourish.

We know that life in that tiny windswept village was a far cry from this idealized version. When John and Priscilla were first married in 1623 life was a constant struggle. After years of hardship, however, the settlers were able to adapt to their new way of life and prosper.

For our Pilgrim dinner we go beyond the early days of the Plymouth colony. John and Priscilla are about to enjoy the bounty of a good harvest and celebrate the success of their new life. Their dinner reflects the staples of the early New England larder: corn, cranberries, turkey, and pumpkin.

Secure in her small wooden house, Priscilla prepares dinner over the blazing fire of an open hearth. The thick oak table is set with hand turned pottery and pewter plates. Large tankards of cider await the evening meal.

From the cauldron hanging over the fire Priscilla ladles hot clam chowder into earthenware cups. In the warming oven waits a pan of turkey and cornbread stuffing covered with a light Madeira sauce. To end the meal a spicy pumpkin pie baked earlier in the day will be brought to the table.

Thus we might see Priscilla and John, pausing to reflect on their accomplishments and looking ahead with hope to the future.

New England Clam Chowder

The sandy shores of Cape Cod Bay bordering the Pilgrim settlement provided abundant shellfish. Clams, scallops, lobsters, and oysters frequently appeared on the colonial table. Clam chowder prepared in the New England style has a distinctive reputation for its rich white creamy broth.

½" cube salt pork, minced
1   cup clam juice
2   small potatoes, cubed
1   medium onion, chopped
6   ounces minced clams
1   cup light cream
pinch white pepper

In medium-size saucepan, brown minced salt pork. Remove browned bits and discard.

Pour clam juice into saucepan. Add potatoes and onion. Cook until potatoes are tender. Add clams, light cream, and pepper. Bring just to boiling point and then reduce heat to low. Simmer for 15-20 minutes.

This will make a thin chowder. If you would like a thicker chowder, simmer for 30 minutes longer.

Turkey Cutlets with Cornbread Stuffing and Madeira Sauce

The forests of New England were once filled with wild fowl. Except for this plentiful source there was very little meat for the first colonists. Turkey as we know it is far different from the stringy bird the Pilgrims knew. Today turkeys are specially bred for flavor and tenderness. Prepackaged turkey cutlets, thin scallops of breast meat, are available for quick cooking or when a whole bird is just too much.

 1 *pound turkey cutlets*
 3 *tablespoons all-purpose flour*
 3 *tablespoons butter*
 ¼ *teaspoon salt*
 pinch pepper

Wash cutlets and pat dry. Coat turkey with flour mixed with salt and pepper. Melt butter in medium-size frying pan. Sauté cutlets until they are light brown on both sides. Transfer to a pan which has been lined with cornbread stuffing.

Madeira Sauce
 ½ *cup Madeira*
 1½ *cups chicken bouillon*
 2 *tablespoons all-purpose flour*
 2 *tablespoons butter*

After removing turkey cutlets from pan, deglaze it with ½ cup Madeira. Add bouillon and stir well. Set aside.

 In a separate pan, melt butter and flour over medium heat. Stir with a wire whisk until all the flour has been incorporated into the butter. Add the liquid from the browning pan and whisk mixture until it is smooth. Cook over medium heat stirring constantly until sauce thickens. Pour over cutlets which have been arranged on cornbread stuffing and bake for 30 minutes at 350°F.

Stuffing

½ small loaf cornbread
½ pound ground sausage meat, browned and drained
1 small onion, chopped
2 tablespoons butter
2 teaspoons parsley
¼ teaspoon sage
¼ teaspoon salt
⅛ teaspoon pepper
1 egg, beaten
½ cup chicken bouillon

Sauté chopped onion in butter until it is translucent. Add sausage, parsley, sage, salt, and pepper. Cook briefly.

Crumble cornbread into a medium bowl. Add sausage mixture, beaten egg, and chicken broth. Toss until the liquid is evenly distributed.

Cornbread For Stuffing

Corn, another gift of the new world, was quickly adopted by the Pilgrims. Learning from the Indians, early cooks found corn ground into meal a valuable addition to their provisions. One popular adaptation, the Journey or Johnny Cake, was made by mixing finely ground meal with scalded milk and then, like pancakes, frying the mixture over an open fire. Another was cornbread, carefully baked above the hearth in a small brick oven.

This cornbread recipe is really best used for stuffing as it contains no sugar. However, if you like things a little less sweet, it is quite good when toasted and spread with butter and jam.

¾ cup all-purpose flour
¼ cup cornmeal
2 teaspoons baking powder
¼ teaspoon salt
½ cup milk
1 egg
⅛ cup vegetable oil

Preheat oven to 400°F. Combine all ingredients until just moistened. Pour into greased 8-inch loaf pan.

Bake 20 minutes at 400°F.

Cranberry Compote

Cranberries are one of the most popular native American fruits. In the early 1600's these bright red berries grew wild in the marshy areas around the Plymouth village. Early settlers in New England followed the Indian practice of cooking them in maple sugar and honey. In this tradition we offer a slightly different version of sweetened cranberries cooked with pears and dried fruit.

This compote is at its best if prepared 1 to 2 days before serving. This allows the flavors to meld and the pears to take on the bright red hue of the cranberry juice.

1 ½ cups cranberries
1   pear (large firm)
¼   cup raisins
½   lemon, sliced thin
¾   cup water
¾   cup brown sugar, firmly packed
¼   teaspoon cinnamon

Wash cranberries in cold water and pick out stems. Peel pear. Remove core and cut into eight sections.

Place all fruits in heavy saucepant. Add sugar, water and cinnamon. Cover and cook slowly over low heat for 30 minutes.

Remove from heat. Discard lemon slices. Transfer cooked fruit and juice to a covered container and store in the refrigerator. This compote may be served cold or at room temperature.

Pumpkin Pie

Pumpkins have been a part of American cooking since early colonial times. Probably native to Central America pumpkins were a staple of the North American Indian diet in the 1600's. Grown extensively they were prepared in a variety of ways. They could be boiled, baked, dried or ground into meal.

Priscilla's pie might have been prepared by hollowing out the center of a pumpkins and filling it with milk, spices and a sweetner. Our pie is a twentieth century version — complete with crust, creamy center, and crunchy praline topping.

Pie Crust
1 ¼ cups all-purpose flour
1   teaspoon sugar
½   teaspoon salt
3   tablespoons ice water
4   tablespoons vegetable shortening, chilled
2   tablespoons sweet butter, chilled

Sift flour, sugar, and salt into mixing bowl. Add chilled shortening and butter. Blend quickly with fingertips or pastry blender until mixture resembles a coarse meal.

Add ice water 1 tablespoon at a time. Toss with a fork. Add more water if needed to hold dough together. Form into a ball. Wrap in waxed paper and chill one hour, before rolling out on a floured surface.

Makes 1- 9" pie crust.

Glaze
1   tablespoon currant jelly
1   teaspoon brandy

In small saucepan, melt jelly over medium heat. Add brandy and blend well. Brush on prepared, unbaked pie shell.

Filling

1 ½ cups mashed pumpkin
1   cup light cream
¾   cup brown sugar, firmly packed
2   eggs
½   teaspoon ground cinnamon
½   teaspoon ginger
¼   teaspoon nutmeg
⅛   teaspoon ground cloves
½   teaspoon salt

Preheat oven to 425°F. In a medium bowl, combine pumpkin with rest of ingredients. Beat until smooth. Pour into glazed pie shell. Bake at 425°F. for 10 minutes. Reduce heat to 350°F. and bake for 45 minutes or until a knife inserted in the center comes out clean. Remove from oven and cool.

Topping

½   cup sugar
½   cup walnuts, chopped

In a small saucepan, cook sugar slowly over medium high heat until sugar melts and forms a syrup. Stir constantly. Fold in chopped nuts. Remove from heat and quickly spread onto well greased baking sheet. Cool completely. When hard, place walnut brittle in a plastic bag. Wrap in a dish towel and crush with a mallet until crumbly. Sprinkle over top of cooled pie. Chill until serving time.

TOKUBEI
AND
OHATSU

It is night. In the hushed garden of a Japanese shrine, two desperate lovers choose to join their ancestors rather than face this life without each other. They embrace the spirits of the afterworld and begin the journey to the Mountain of Death. So ends the story of Tokubei and Ohatsu, the hero and heroine of the drama, "The Love Suicides at Sonezaki", written by the eighteenth century Japanese playwright Monzaemon Chikamatsu.

First performed in the early 1700's, this formal puppet drama (Bunraku) is a portrayal of a tragic Japanese love story. Like others written by Chikamatsu it was modeled on a real life tragedy . . .

Tokubei, a clerk in a soy shop in Osaka, is in love with Ohatsu, a courtesan from a local tea house. For many years they have dreamed about life together. They wish to marry but the obstacles to such a union are insurmountable. Tokubei's uncle has arranged a marriage for him which he will not accept. He must therefore return the dowry money that has already been paid. Unfortunately, he is unable to do so because he has loaned it to a friend, a man who now denies the debt. Tokubei feels humiliated, believing his honor is lost.

Ohatsu feels the pain of her lover's desperation. She aches with the knowledge that she is the cause of it. Passionately she proclaims her own love and vows that they will be together, if not in this world then in the next.

One of the most beautiful parts of this play is the poetry at the conclusion. Movingly our ill-fated lovers bid farewell to the beauty around them. Their words echo the Japanese awareness of the ephemeral nature of existence. How fast time passes, how fleeting the joys and sorrows of this life.

This general attitude toward life influences many aspects of Japanese culture. We see it in the simplicity of their flower arrangements where a single flower may be the focal point of our attention. We see it again in the ritual of the tea ceremony and in the artistry evident in the presentation of their foods. Color, shape, and arrangement are as important as taste. A meal must appeal to all of the senses.

Many evenings Tokubei and Ohatsu dined behind the sliding screens of the tea house. There dressed in silk kimonos, seated before low lacquered tables, they enjoyed the pleasures of Osaka's cuisine. Tangy beef teriyaki, feather-light tempura shrimp and vegetables and, of course, rice were served with small cups of warm saki, and the night was filled with their whispers of desire and hope.

Cucumber Salad

Thin crunchy slices of cucumber are a refreshing beginning to this dinner. Thought to have been grown as far back as 7750 B.C. in ancient Indonesia, cucumbers are now successfully grown in many parts of the world.

1   cucumber
½   teaspoon salt
2   tablespoons Chinese rice vinegar
1   teaspoon sugar
1   teaspoon soy sauce
1   tablespoon finely chopped scallions
pinch pepper

Wash and slice unpeeled cucumber into paper thin slices. Place in a small bowl and sprinkle with salt. Cover and place a weight on top of the cucumbers to press out excess moisture. Let stand for 1 hour.

Drain cucumbers and squeeze dry. In a serving bowl combine all ingredients and toss gently. Chill until serving time.

Beef Teriyaki

Teriyaki sauce can be used to marinate meat, fish or poultry. These thin strips of beef have a pleasant tang to them. Watch carefully while broiling.

4   ounces sirloin beef tips
1   tablespoon saki or Chinese cooking wine
3   tablespoons soy sauce
½   teaspoon sugar
1   tablespoon sesame oil
1   clove garlic, minced
½   teaspoon minced fresh ginger root

Slice beef into thin strips. Combine rest of ingredients to form marinade. Add beef and allow to marinate at room temperature for ½ hour. Or prepare early in day and refrigerate.

Using thin bamboo sticks, lace meat so that it is flat and stretches out end to end. Place in broiling pan and broil for 3 minutes on each side. Serve immediately.

Shrimp and Vegetable Tempura

The success of a tempura rests on the thin batter which lightly veils the fish and vegetables and quick frying in hot oil. It is important to use very hot oil for this dish or the vegetables will be soggy. If you prepare vegetables early, store them in cold water and pat dry before dipping in batter.

One of the delights of Japanese cooking is seeing it prepared on the table in front of you. If you have an electric wok or fondue dish you can cook this dish at the table in your own home.

Batter
1   egg white
½   cup sifted all-purpose flour
2   tablespoons cornstarch
½   cup cold water

Beat egg white and cold water. Sift flour and cornstarch into egg mixture. Mix lightly with a whisk. Do not overmix as you want the batter to be light.

4   jumbo shrimp, peeled and deveined
4   slices each of yam, summer squash, zucchini, peeled
4   large mushrooms
4   cups peanut oil

Heat oil. With a fondue fork or prongs dip shrimp and vegetables into batter one at a time and place in hot oil. Do not crowd. Cook until outer coating is crisp. Serve with tempura sauce.

Tempura sauce
¼   cup dashi (chicken or fish stock or bouillon)
1   tablespoon soy sauce (shoyu)
1   tablesppon rice wine (saki)
freshly grated ginger root for extra zest

Rice with Vegetables

Rice is one of the two most important food crops in the world. (The other being wheat.) In some places it is virtually the only food which sustains life. Evidence has been found which suggests that even as early as 3500 B.C. rice was eaten in Thailand and other Indonesian countries. It is possible that rice came to Japan from China where it had been cultivated since 2800 B.C. In Japan it gained steadily in importance as part of the diet and as a symbol of wealth. In fact, in feudal times a man's wealth was measured by how many pounds of rice were produced per acre on his land. Samurai were also paid with rice.

Today the Japanese still eat large quantities of rice with each meal and are likely to feel dissatisfied if no rice is offered.

½   cup uncooked white rice
1 ¼ cups water
¼   cup bamboo shoots
1   large mushroom, chopped
½   cup firmly packed fresh spinach, washed, patted dry and chopped
¼   cup Chinese cabbage, chopped (If you cannot find Chinese cabbage, green cabbage will do just as well.)
2   tablespoons peanut oil
1   tablespoon soy sauce
1   tablespoon rice wine (saki)

Cook rice in 1 ½ cups boiling water. Allow to cool.

In a medium-size frying pan, heat the peanut oil. Add bamboo shoots, mushroom, spinach, and cabbage. Stir fry for a few minutes until the cabbage and spinach are limp. Add the cooked rice, soy sauce, and rice wine. Blend thoroughly.

Rice may be kept warm in an oven proof dish.

Pineapple Sherbet

Whether the pineapple was known to the ancient Egyptians or not, it was first discovered by modern man in 1493 on the island of Guadeloupe. Since then it has spread to Europe, Hawaii, and the Far East. Fresh pineapple is available year round and gives this sherbet a delightfully refreshing taste.

    2   cups puréed pineapple
    ¾   cup granulated sugar
    ½   cup milk

Combine pineapple purée, sugar, and milk. Blend well. Pour into a freezer tray and freeze until mushy. Transfer to a medium bowl and beat with a mixer until creamy. Return to freezer until firm.

PAO YU
AND
TAI YU

From the pen of the Chinese author, Tsao Hsueh-chin, comes the novel *Dream of the Red Chamber*. Rooted in the era of the Ch'ing Dynasty (1600 to 1844) and set in the Far Eastern city of Peking, it tells of two young people, Pao yu and Tai yu. From deep within the mystical realms of Buddhism and Taoism their magical love story unfolds. It is not a simple story but one filled with intrigue and the courtly manners of a time long past in Chinese history. Indeed, historians consider it to be one of the greatest Chinese novels ever written.

The story begins in the Dome of Heaven, a far off place somewhere between what is real and unreal. There, amid cloud wrapped mountains and mist covered seas the Stone, a mythological figure, struggles with his fate. Destined to dwell within the divine world, endowed with supernatural powers, the Stone feels a yearning for life in the Red Dust (the mortal world). The mysteries of mortality, the pleasure, pain, and sorrow of life, beckon to him.

The Stone comes to earth in the form of a young man — Pao yu. He is blessed with a symbol of importance and character in the shape of a fine column of jade which he wears always. Pao yu is permitted to partake of the rituals of a full life. While he is still young he meets Tai yu, an orphaned maiden. They fall deeply in love and plan to marry. But, as is typical of that matriarchal society, Pao yu's aunts have different plans for him. In an ingenious charade they deceive him by marrying him to a woman they believe more proper for his station in life. Overwhelmed by sadness Tai yu, his beloved, dies, apparently from a broken heart. Pao yu finds the courage to go on despite his grief.

[93]

As a mortal he still seeks to experience the joys of life. In the end, though, he finds the pleasure is far outweighed by the sorrow and he returns to the Great Mythical Mountain, disillusioned and unfulfilled.

One of life's pleasures for Pao yu must have been eating, for in the Chinese culture cooking has long been valued as an art. In fact Confucius taught that the appreciation of good food was part of a full life.

This dinner is inspired by the lovers in this story. Like them you, too, can follow the Chinese ideal of eating and sharing pleasure. Choosing pork and chicken, the two most often used meats in Chinese cooking, we prepare several dishes in the Peking manner. Although rice is a staple in China, in this region wheat flour predominates. Thus we offer a lo mein (noodle) dish to accompany the chicken with cashews. Start with Peking-style dumplings and spare ribs and your joy will be assured.

Chicken with Cashews

The emphasis in Chinese cooking is on the harmonious mixing of ingredients. This dish is a delightful contrast of textures from the moist plump pieces of chicken to the crunchy pea pods and cashews.

Chicken Marinade
1	pound chicken breasts, deboned, cubed
1	tablespoon soy sauce
2	tablespoons Chinese rice wine
1	teaspoon sesame oil
1½	teaspoons cornstarch

Vegetables
¼	pound snow peas
2	large mushrooms
1	tablespoon minced scallion
1	clove garlic, minced
1	teaspoon minced fresh ginger root

Seasonings
⅓	cup chicken bouillon
1	tablespoon Chinese rice wine
2	tablespoon soy sauce
2	teaspoons sugar
½	teaspoon sesame oil
1	teaspoon rice vinegar
1	teaspoon cornstarch
¼	cup roasted unsalted cashews
¼	cup peanut oil

The first thing to do is marinate the chicken. Combine the soy sauce, rice wine, sesame oil, and cornstarch in a small bowl. Remove the skin and bones from the chicken breasts and cube the meat. Add the chicken to the marinade and let stand at room temperature for 20 minutes.

Meanwhile prepare the vegetables. Wash and drain snow peas and remove ends. Wash mushrooms and pat dry. Slice them and set both vegetables aside. Mince scallions, garlic, and ginger root.

For ease in cooking combine the "seasonings" in a bowl and have just that ready before you begin cooking the chicken.

Just before you are ready to sit down to dinner, pour ¼ cup peanut oil into a wok or large frying pan. Set over high heat. Brown chicken in hot oil for about 2 minutes. Add scallions, garlic, and ginger. Cook for 1 minute. Add "seasonings" and cook for 2 to 3 minutes until the sauce thickens. Add vegetables and cook until the mushrooms are firm. Turn out onto a platter and serve immediately.

Peking Style Ravioli

Ravioli, an international favorite, are prepared differently in many countries and called by different names. Nevertheless, the idea of filling circles of dough with a meat mixture remains the same. These dough wrapped bits of pork are well seasoned with Chinese spices. They are then steamed and fried in a unique manner.

¼   pound lean ground pork
¼   cup finely chopped Chinese cabbage
1   tablespoon finely minced scallions
1   teaspoon soy sauce
1   teaspoon Chinese rice wine
¼   teaspoon minced fresh ginger root
⅛   teaspoon Five Spice powder
⅛   teaspoon salt
pinch pepper
1   teaspoon sesame oil
¼   teaspoon minced garlic
4   tablespoons peanut oil
24   round ravioli wrappers*

Chop vegetables and mix well with ground pork. Add all other ingredients except peanut oil and mix well. The best way to do this is with your fingers. Sprinkle a large dinner plate with flour so that the dumplings will not stick.

When using prepackaged wrappers, we found it advantageous to use two for each dumpling. By moistening one wrapper with water and covering it with a second, the dumplings held together better during cooking. To assemble, place double wrapper on counter. Moisten outer edge with water. Place 1 teaspoon of filling in the center. Fold over so that you form a half moon. Pinch the moistened edges together so that they stick all the way around. If you don't seal the ravioli properly, they may fall apart during cooking. When you are finished preparing the ravioli, cover them with a damp towel and place in the refrigerator (if you are not going to cook them right away).

To cook, place 2 tablespoons of peanut oil in a large frying pan. Turn heat to medium-high. When oil is hot, add the ravioli so that they are not touching. Cook for 2 to 3 minutes until the underside is browned. Turn and brown on the other side.

Add ½ cup hot water. Lower heat, cover and cook for 10 minutes. (Be sure to loosen the ravioli with a spatula at least once after adding the water to avoid sticking.) Uncover and pour off any remaining water. Add 2 tablespoons of peanut oil to pan and cook again uncovered for 2 to 3 minutes. Serve immediately with Chinese style duck sauce if you desire.

*Note: Wrappers are available in Oriental markets.

Spareribs

Anyone who has eaten Chinese food undoubtedly loves spareribs. These meaty, slightly sweet tasting ribs will be a favorite of yours too.

¾   pound baby pork spare ribs
2   tablespoons soy sauce
2   tablespoons plum sauce or honey
1   tablespoon Chinese rice wine

Combine all ingredients. Marinate the ribs for at least one hour or earlier in the day. To cook, place on broiling pan and baste with marinade. Turn oven to broil and place pan approximately 8 inches from heat source. Broil for 7 to 8 minutes on each side occasionally brushing with marinade. Watch carefully so the ribs don't burn. If you like, serve with additional plum sauce.

Lo Mein

Noodles are very popular in China especially in the Northern provinces. They may be prepared for any meal using a large variety of ingredients. Recently Chinese noodles have been made available in supermarkets in addition to specialty shops. Thus you can enjoy them in your own dining room. If you cannot find Chinese noodles, thin style linguini makes a good substitute.

8	ounces Chinese noodles
2	quarts boiling water
½	teaspoon salt
2	tablespoons sesame oil
2	tablespoons minced scallions
1	teaspoon finely minced fresh ginger root
¼	cup sliced water chestnuts
½	cup chicken bouillon
1	tablespoon Chinese rice wine
2	tablespoons soy sauce
1	clove garlic, minced

Bring water and salt to boil. Add noodles and cook for 5 minutes even though the Chinese noodles will say "cooked." Drain.

In a large frying pan, sauté scallions and garlic in sesame oil over medium heat for 1 to 2 minutes. Add ginger root, soy sauce, wine, and bouillon. Simmer for 5 minutes. Drain water chestnuts and add to mixture. Add noodles and toss well. Cook for 1 to 2 minutes until noodles are hot. Serve immediately.

Honey Bananas

This is a simplified version of the classic Peking honey bananas. Instead of caramelizing the fried bananas, we suggest a honey-wine sauce which is warmed and spooned over the cooked fruit. Allow the fritters to crisp before covering with the sauce.

1	large or 2 small bananas
¼	cup sifted all-purpose flour
2	tablespoons cornstarch
1	egg white, beaten until frothy
2	tablespoons sugar
¼	cup cold water
1	cup peanut oil
¼	cup honey
1	tablespoon plum wine or port

Cut banana in half the long way and then into large chunks. Prepare the batter of flour, cornstarch, egg white, sugar, and water.

In a wok or medium-size frying pan, heat oil over high heat. Coat chunks of banana well with batter and let stand while oil is heating. Be sure that oil is very hot or fritters will be soggy. Meanwhile warm honey and wine in a small saucepan.

Place bananas in hot oil being careful to leave a space between them. Brown on both sides. Remove from oil and drain on paper towels. After a few moments place fritters on a serving plate and spoon sauce over them.

FRANCISCO GOYA
AND
THE DUCHESS OF ALBA

Time has not dimmed the controversy inspired by the artist Francisco de Goya and Maria Teresa, the Duchess of Alba. Even though more than one hundred years have passed, an air of mystery still surrounds the liaison between them. People may still whisper about them but only Goya and the Duchess know the truth of their love affair. In public they shared only a passion for bullfighting but in private, who can say? Accounts of the era tell us that in the year 1796, at the age of fifty and nearly deaf, a desperate Goya, in search of inspiration, travelled to Sanlúcar in southern Spain. There he found what he was seeking in the beautiful and desirable Duchess of Alba. With patent disregard for convention he abandoned his family. With a new vitality, he devoted himself to this alluring woman.

As a painter Goya was able to capture on canvas Maria Teresa's spirit and fire. One of his most famous paintings, *The Duchess of Alba*, seems to reveal to us the depth of his love. The Spanish noblewoman stands imperiously, her back to the sea, clad in a long flowing black dress and mantilla. With one hand she points almost defiantly to the sand at her feet, where are written the words, "Solamente Goya," "Only Goya."

Indeed the sand and the sea were everywhere around them in this Andalusian province. Sanlúcar, with its white washed houses and red tiled roofs throbbed with sultry heat and the rousing tempo of Flamenco music. The smell of sun drenched flowers and fragrant orange and lemon groves filled their senses. Amid this Mediterranean splendor Goya and Maria Teresa sought privacy in the Duchess's Moorish estate.

As the sun hovers on the horizon and the blue twilight approaches, they share a glass of sherry. In the kitchen, preparations are being made for an appetizing regional meal. Unlike the hot and spicy food we associate with Mexican cooking, Spanish cooks of this area combine herbs and spices to season light, easily digestible dishes, a necessary concession to the high temperatures which characterize the Sanlúcar summer.

This evening the first course will be gazpacho, a soup made from tomatoes, garlic, and oil. The main course will be chunks of white fish, lightly breaded and fried, and sprinkled with fresh lemon juice. Dessert is a lemon-coconut tart, a slight diversion from the traditional flan which is so popular in Spain.

Gazpacho

This crisp cool soup offers a light refreshing counterpoint to the sultry summer heat of Andalusia. The subtle spices stimulate the palate without being overpowering.

We are fortunate today to have access to the refrigerator and blender to aid in the preparation of this soup. In the eighteenth century the Andalusian cook would have used a mortar and pestle to crush the aromatic vegetables. Then the finished gazpacho would have been poured into a clay bowl and kept cool in the shade. At serving time the garniture would represent the freshest vegetables available on that day.

3	medium tomatoes
1	medium cucumber
½	red pepper
1	teaspoon chopped pimento
1	cup water
½	clove garlic, minced
½	medium onion, chopped fine
¾	teaspoon salt
2	tablespoons wine vinegar
1	cup crusty white bread crumbs
2	tablespoons olive oil
⅛	teaspoon pepper
1	small can tomato juice (5 ½ -ounces)

Garnitures
chopped hard cooked eggs
chopped green pepper
chopped scallions

Peel and seed tomatoes and cucumber. Cut into chunks. Seed and coarsely chop red pepper. In a blender, purée tomatoes, cucumber, onion, and garlic until smooth. Add rest of ingredients and blend well. Chill.

When ready to serve pour mixture into chilled bowls. Serve with garnitures.

Fried Fish

The smell of fish frying fills the air along the Mediterranean sea coast. In small towns the catch of the day is frequently the evening meal. Lightly coated with flour and fried in olive oil, these tender fillets are one of the most popular foods of the Spanish coastal province of Andalusia.

> 12 ounces of white fish fillets, such as flounder, sole, halibut
>   or haddock
> flour for dredging
> ¼ teaspoon salt
> pinch pepper
> 1 cup olive oil
> lemon wedges

Mix flour, salt, and pepper. Cut fish into serving pieces and coat with seasoned flour. In a medium frying pan, heat oil until it is very hot but not smoking. Brown fish on both sides. Drain on paper towel. Place on serving dish surrounded by lemon wedges.

Andalusian Rice Salad

Spaniards rely heavily on rice as an accompaniment to their meals. This cold rice salad combines olives, pimentos, and spicy ham, all favorites in this region. When preparing this dish be sure to mix all ingredients while the rice is hot. Then chill well until serving time.

½   cup uncooked rice
1½ cups water
4   ounces marinated mushrooms*
1   scallion, minced including green top
1   ounce hot ham, cut into small pieces
8   medium black olives, sliced
1½ tablespoons chopped pimentos
1   tablespoon chopped parsley
salt
pepper

Bring water to boil. Stir in rice. Cover and simmer over low heat until all the water is absorbed (20 to 25 minutes). Transfer rice to a medium-size bowl. Add marinated mushrooms with liquid, scallions, ham, olives, pimentos, and parsley.

   Season with salt and pepper to taste. (Remember the ham, mushrooms and olives are already salty.) Chill.

*Marinated Mushrooms
4   ounces white mushrooms
2   tablespoons olive oil
¼   cup dressing (2 tablespoons olive oil + 1 tablespoon
    white vinegar)
1   teaspoon chopped parsley
pinch salt
pinch pepper
dash garlic powder

Wash mushrooms and carefully pat dry. Slice mushrooms and sauté in olive oil for 2 to 3 minutes. In a small bowl, combine all other ingredients. Stir in sautéed mushrooms.

Lemon-Coconut Tart

The flan is a frequent dessert in Spanish-speaking countries. It usually is served in the manner of the French Crème Caramel, a crustless, caramelized vanilla flavored custard. We have prepared a tart which is similar to a flan but easier to make. Its tangy, smooth texture is a pleasant contrast to the sweet crunch of the coconut crust.

Toasted coconut crust
1   cup coconut (sweetened)
2   tablespoons butter, melted

To toast coconut, spread on a baking sheet in a thin layer. Bake at 350°F. for approximately 5 to 7 minutes, stirring occasionally. Watch carefully to avoid scorching. When coconut is a light brown, transfer to a small bowl. Add melted butter and mix thoroughly. Press onto the bottom and ½-inch up the side of a buttered 8-inch spring form pan. Set aside.

Filling

8   ounces cream cheese
    (not whipped)
½   cup granulated sugar
2   eggs
¼   cup light cream
1   tablespoon lemon juice
¼   teaspoon grated lemon rind
1   tablespoon all-purpose flour

Topping

½   cup sour cream
1   tablespoon lemon juice
¼   teaspoon vanilla extract

In the large bowl of an electric mixer, combine cream cheese and sugar and beat well. Add remaining ingredients and beat until the mixture is smooth and there are no lumps of cream cheese. Pour into prepared coconut crust.

Bake in preheated 400°F. oven for 20 minutes. Remove from oven and place on a wire rack for 10 minutes. Meanwhile, combine sour cream, lemon juice, and vanilla extract. Spread over entire top of tart. Return pan to oven and bake for 10 minutes more. Remove from oven and cool on a wire rack. Tart may be served at room temperature or chilled.

NAPOLEON
AND
JOSEPHINE

From the very first time they met in the house on the Rue Chantereine in Paris there was a mysterious spark of electricity between Napoleon Bonaparte and Josephine de Beauharnais.

As a child on the island of Martinique, Josephine had lived a life free from turmoil and filled with laughter. Later, as a young girl, she traveled to France. There misfortune and an unhappy first marriage tempered her gaiety and made her cautious. When she met Napoleon, Josephine immediately recognized the advantages an alliance with him could bring. Even though part of her yearned for the security of marriage she was afraid of losing her treasured freedom to do as she pleased. Still, here was a man who seemed to love her and want her as a companion in his climb to fame.

To the young officer Josephine appeared to be small and delicate. No other woman fascinated him in quite the same way. He seemed to find a kindred spirit in her. Napoleon's early years in France had given him a strong character and filled him with intense ambition. He had been born in Corsica but had spent many years in French schools, never quite feeling accepted as an equal. In spite of this, he studied hard and earned a scholarship to the École Militaire in Paris. There he became a brilliant artillery strategist, an accomplishment which was to serve him well in the future.

Once he met Josephine, Napoleon was totally captivated and anxious to marry. But Josephine was not easily persuaded. Napoleon wooed her with sentimental gifts and passionate letters. His consuming love became legendary. Desperately the now self-assured, steely eyed young man yearned for this woman to be his alone and to share in his life completely.

Finally, in 1796, Josephine capitulated to the pleas of the man who had pursued her so unceasingly. This made Napoleon supremely happy. They complemented each other perfectly. She was the consummate hostess and he a recognized military expert with a flair for politics. Together they conquered the French. In 1804, they were welcomed as Emperor and Empress.

At times, when the burdens of state affairs became too great, Napoleon and Josephine retreated to their country estate, Malmaison. This magnificent estate boasted not only a large elegant mansion but also hundreds of lush fertile acres. Amid flourishing flower gardens, honeycombed with paths, grottoes, and fountains, the Emperor and Empress lived royally. Josephine was able to indulge in several extravagant ventures. Among them was a hothouse filled with exotic flowers. In addition she also was able to grow pineapples, bananas, mangoes, and dwarf fruit trees. Their bounty frequently graced the dining table.

On balmy spring and summer evenings it was not unusual for Napoleon and Josephine to dine alfresco on the broad green lawn which bordered the chateau's facade. The warm evening air carried the scents of freshly cut grass and fragrant blossoms. Peering through the multipaned french windows one might see a small, linen-covered table set with hand-cut crystal and fine French porcelain. Soon the imperial lovers would dine à deux on crab stuffed mushrooms, tender scallops of veal in a creamy tarragon sauce, and a golden puffed potato soufflé. A three-layered hazelnut gateau with coffee buttercream would provide the crowning touch for this very special dinner.

Crab Stuffed Mushrooms

This first course combines two widely eaten foods into one luscious dish. Crabs are found just about everywhere in the world where there is water (even on land in some places). Amazingly enough, every one of the 4400 species is edible.

Who knows how long mushrooms have been eaten and appreciated for their nutritive value. Hippocrates utilized them as food and for their medicinal attributes. Today they are so popular that some are cultivated by artificial means.

    8   large mushrooms (1 ½ to 2 inches)
    1   tablespoon finely chopped shallot
    2   tablesppons butter
    2   tablesppons fine dry bread crumbs
    ¼   cup crab meat
    1   teaspoon chopped parsley
    pinch pepper

Rinse crab meat under cold water and drain. Pick over meat for any traces of shell.

Carefully remove stems from mushrooms and chop fine. Melt butter. Add stems and shallots and cook until shallots are translucent. Remove from heat. Add crab meat, bread crumbs, parsley, and pepper. Stir until blended. Fill mushrooms by dividing mixture evenly. Bake on cookie sheet in preheated 350°F. oven for 15 minutes. Serve hot.

Veal with Tarragon and Cream

Veal has earned the reputation as a very elegant main course. Thinly sliced, it can be cooked quickly and deliciously with a host of different seasonings. We have chosen tarragon, which has a wonderful aroma and excellent flavor, as a seasoning. You will find that it gives the veal a unique taste without very many other ingredients.

¾   *pound scallops of veal*
1   *tablespoon flour*
2   *tablespoons butter*
½   *cup dry white wine*
½   *cup light cream*
1   *teaspoon Dijon style mustard*
⅛   *teaspoon salt*
pinch pepper
½   *teaspoon dried tarragon, crushed*

Place veal between two sheets of wax paper and pound until thin to tenderize meat. Coat evenly with flour.

In a large frying pan, melt butter over low-medium heat. Sauté veal for 3 to 4 minutes on each side. Remove veal from pan and set aside.

Add wine to pan and scrape drippings from bottom with a spatula. Cook for 3 minutes over low heat. Slowly add light cream to mixture, stirring constantly. Don't worry if the cream appears to curdle. Assuming the cream is fresh the sauce will be smooth in the end. Add mustard, salt, pepper, and tarragon and continue to cook, stirring constantly. When sauce is smooth, return veal to pan and heat thoroughly. Serve immediately.

Potato Soufflé

Delightful egg based creations dramatically puffed into soufflés can be part of any meal. They can be flavored with meats, vegetables, fruits, and countless other ingredients.

In France, when it was first introduced, the potato was deemed food for the riff-raff and thought to be unhealthy. By the late 1700's though, it was an accepted part of everyone's diet.

⅔   cup mashed potatoes
1½   tablespoons butter
1½   tablespoons all-purpose flour
½   cup milk
2   eggs, separated
½   teaspoon salt
⅛   teaspoon cayenne pepper

Preheat oven to 375°F. Melt butter over low heat. Add flour and stir with a wire whisk until all the flour is incorporated into the butter. Add milk, stirring constantly, until the mixture is smooth and begins to thicken. Remove from heat and cool slightly.

Add egg yolks one at a time, stirring constantly. Add seasonings and potatoes. Mix well. Beat egg whites until stiff and carefully fold into potato mixture.

Pour into ungreased soufflé dish and bake at 375°F. for 20 to 25 minutes. Remove from oven and serve at once.

Glazed Carrots

As an edible root, carrots probably were eaten even before man began cultivating food. Fresh carrots have a rather sweet taste which makes them a very popular vegetable. In addition they have been shown to contribute actively to good health. Glazing carrots in this manner makes them elegant enough for an emperor's table.

½   pound carrots
1   cup beef bouillon
3   tablespoons butter
1   teaspoon granulated sugar
¼   teaspoon salt
⅛   teaspoon pepper

Clean carrots. Slice them in quarters lengthwise and then into 2-inch sticks.

In a medium-size saucepan, combine bouillon, butter, sugar, salt, and pepper over medium heat. Cook briefly. Add carrots. Cover and cook over low heat for 20 minutes or until carrots are tender.

Carrots may be prepared early in the day and reheated just before serving.

Hazelnut Gateau

This gateau is a magnificent creation guaranteed to show off your culinary abilities.

Gateau

4   eggs (at room temperature), separated
4   tablespoons sweet butter, softened
¾   cup granulated sugar
1   teaspoon vanilla extract
3   tablespoons fine dry bread crumbs
⅓   cup hazelnuts, ground

Apricot Filling

2   tablespoons apricot preserves
1   teaspoon Grand Marnier liqueur

Coffee Buttercream

4   tablespoons sweet butter, softened
2   cups confectioners' sugar
2   tablespoons light cream
1   teaspoon instant coffee (powdered) dissolved in 2 tablespoons boiling water

Preheat oven to 350°F. Butter a 9" by 13" baking pan and line the bottom with wax paper. Butter the paper.

In a large mixing bowl, at medium speed, beat egg yolks, butter, and sugar until fluffy and lemon colored. Add vanilla and bread crumbs and beat at high speed for 2 minutes. Fold in hazelnuts.

In a separate bowl beat egg whites until stiff. Stir ¼ of the egg whites into the hazelnut batter to lighten it. Then carefully fold in the balance of the egg whites. Pour into prepared pan and distribute evenly. Bake 12 to 15 minutes. Top should be a light brown. Cake will shrink away from sides of pan. Cool in pan for 5 minutes. Then invert on wire rack, carefully remove wax paper and cool completely. Cut into 3 even layers.

Blend filling ingredients and set aside.

Beat sugar and butter until butter can no longer be seen. Add coffee and cream. Beat until smooth. If necessary add more cream, a little at a time, until frosting is a spreadable consistency.

To assemble gateau: Place one layer of cake on a serving platter. Brush with ½ the apricot mixture. Spread with a thin layer of buttercream. Repeat with second layer. End with layer of cake. Cover entire cake with frosting and decorate with additional ground hazelnuts.

VICTORIA
AND
ALBERT

Royalty's tradition of arranged marriages rarely produces great lovers. There is, however, one couple that proves an exception to this rule — Queen Victoria and Prince Albert.

Victoria, the daughter of the Duke and Duchess of Kent, was nineteen years old when she came to the English throne. Almost immediately a search began for a suitable husband for the young queen. Where could he be found? More importantly, what man would set aside his own ambitions and place himself in the shadow of a woman?

Indeed there was such a man. Albert, the tall, handsome German Prince of Saxe-Coburg, was an ideal, if somewhat reluctant, suitor. As a well educated and strong minded individual he recognized the difficulties of such a liaison. But the lure of being husband to a queen and the opportunity to exercise a sense of moral duty overcame his misgivings. Ultimately he did consent to be Victoria's husband. She was ecstatic. As a young girl she had met and admired him. Now, as a young woman, she fell in love with him.

Idolized by her people, Victoria possessed a majestic bearing. Perhaps it was this demeanor and her known penchant for etiquette which contributed to the naming of the "Victorian Age." In truth she was a romantic who liked nothing better than to dance the night away with her Albert.

Victoria was madly in love with her husband. Once Albert had established his position, both politically and in Victoria's eyes, their life took on a harmony which lasted until his death. Victoria valued him as her confidential adviser and household administrator. She looked to him for opinions on everything from affairs of state to her dress. Upon his death in 1861 she went into a period of mourning which lasted until her own life ended forty years later.

In their years together Victoria and Albert divided their time between Windsor Castle and Buckingham Palace. In the summers, however, they sought a place in the country, far removed from the formality of court. Even though the pressures of a reigning monarch were always upon them they did find such a place in Scotland. At Balmoral they were able to enjoy the free and informal life style that was impossible anywhere else.

In the day room, filled with Victoria's water colors and Albert's hunting tropies, they shared many pleasurable afternoons. By that time the ritual of high tea was a well established, special part of the day. Fresh from a long walk over the heather-covered hills, Victoria and Albert come in to refresh themselves at a traditional Scottish tea. A serving girl wheels in the gilded tea cart. The highly polished silver tea service glistens in the waning light. On one shelf a chilled crock of buttery potted shrimp sits next to a large tray of tea sandwiches. Below these are several tempting sweets. One plate displays thin slices of fruitcake soaked with Scottish liqueur. Another boasts delicate oatmeal lace baskets filled with strawberry cream. In the center, covered with a fine, linen napkin, is a basket of warm scones needing only fresh sweet butter and jam.

Here, among their personal mementos and bright tartan plaids, Queen Victoria and Prince Albert cherish their moments alone.

Potted Shrimp

The English, a people whose food tends to be uncomplicated, are quite fond of dishes prepared in this way. As in any simple cooking, the quality of the finished product depends on the freshness of the ingredients. This shrimp and butter spread has a creamy texture flavored by the subtle addition of wine and spices.

1	pound shrimp, cleaned and deveined
¼	cup butter
¼	teaspoon dry (powdered) mustard
pinch mace	
¼	teaspoon chervil
2	tablespoons pale dry sherry
½	teaspoon parsley
1	teaspoon lemon juice
1	teaspoon chopped scallion
⅛	teaspoon salt
pinch cayenne pepper	

To cook shrimp, bring one quart of water plus 1 teaspoon salt to a rolling boil. Toss in shrimp. Allow water to come to a boil again and cook shrimp for 2 to 3 minutes or until shrimp are pink. Rinse with cold water. Drain well.

Combine shrimp with remaining ingredients in a blender or food processor and process until consistency of a thick paste. Pack into a crock or small bowl and chill. Serve with thin sliced squares of toast.

Tea Sandwiches

By the eighteenth century the ritual of afternoon tea was well established in England and its environs. Traditionally there were extensive preparations, both in achieving just the right brew and in preparing the accompanying delicacies. Breads, scones, muffins, thin sandwiches with various fillings, fruit cakes, and special tarts were samples of the incredible delights offered.

We suggest the sandwich fillings presented here. They are unique in taste and need only the addition of good quality, freshly baked bread. Remove crusts and cut into triangles for a festive look.

Chicken with curried mayonnaise and raisins

1	whole chicken breast, cooked
2	tablespoons mayonnaise
½	teaspoon curry powder
1	teaspoon water
¼	cup raisins, plumped

Chop chicken finely. In a small bowl, combine the mayonnaise, curry powder, and water. Add chicken and raisins and blend thoroughly. Chill until ready to make sandwiches.

Ham with Stilton cheese

4	ounces boiled or baked ham
2	ounces Stilton cheese, crumbled
1	tablespoon mayonnaise
¼	teaspoon dry mustard

Chop ham into small pieces. Add cheese, mayonnaise, and mustard. Blend well. Refrigerate.

Smoked Salmon with Cream Cheese and Dill
2   *ounces smoked salmon*
3   *ounces cream cheese*
⅛   *teaspoon dill weed*

Cut salmon into small pieces. Blend with softened cream cheese and dill. If mixture is too thick add 1 teaspoon milk.

Egg Salad with Bacon and Chives
2   *eggs, hard boiled, chopped*
3   *strips bacon, cooked, drained and crumbled*
1   *tablespoon mayonnaise*
1   *teaspoon English style mustard*
½   *teaspoon chives, chopped*

Mix all ingredients with a fork. Chill.

Fruitcake

Fruitcake is typical of English cookery and is often featured at an afternoon tea. Once a symbol of a family's prosperity, this rich combination of exotic fruits and nuts is suitable fare for the queen who headed the extensive British Empire for so many years.

Dense and moist, this classic white fruitcake is filled with colorful dried fruits and nuts. It takes on a unique flavor when treated to a liberal dose of the Scottish liqueur Drambuie.

1   *stick sweet butter (½ cup)*
¾   *cup sugar*
3   *eggs*
1   *tablespoon milk*
1¼ *cups sifted all-purpose flour (2 tablespoons reserved)*
½   *teaspoon vanilla extract*
¼   *teaspoon salt*
½   *teaspoon ground mace*
¼   *teaspoon baking powder*
¼   *cup coarsely chopped pecans*
¼   *cup currants*
½   *cup golden raisins*
½   *cup candied cherries*
¼   *cup candied pineapple*
1½ *ounces Drambuie liqueur*

Preheat oven to 300°F. Grease and flour bottom and sides of a 9-inch loaf pan.

Cream butter and sugar. Add eggs one at a time and beat well. Add milk, flour, vanilla, salt, mace, and baking powder. Beat until smooth.

Place all fruit in a large bowl. Toss lightly with 2 tablespoons reserved flour. Add fruit and nuts to batter. Stir gently. Pour batter into prepared loaf pan. Tip batter into corners and up along sides for even baking.

Place on center rack in oven. Bake at 300°F. for 1 hour and 30 minutes. Cool 15 minutes in pan. Remove from pan and cool completely on rack, before drizzling with liqueur. Wrap tightly in foil. Cake will keep for several weeks if wrapping is airtight. After one week add another 1½ ounces of Drambuie.

Scones

It is said that the scone gets its name from the palace in Perthshire where the kings of Scotland were crowned. This sweet version traditionally is served hot, with butter and jam, at tea time.

1   cup + 2 tablespoons all-purpose flour
2   teaspoons baking powder
¼   cup sugar
¼   teaspoon salt
¼   cup butter, softened
1   egg
¼   cup milk

Preheat oven to 400°F. Sift dry ingredients together. Add butter and blend with a pastry fork or finger tips.

Beat egg and milk together lightly. Fold into the flour mixture until just blended. Turn dough out onto floured board. Knead briefly (one minute).

Roll dough into a circle about ½-inch thick. With a sharp knife cut into six triangles. Transfer to a greased and floured cookie sheet. Leave at least two inches between scones.

Bake at 400°F. for 12 to 15 minutes or until scones are a light brown. Remove from oven and serve warm with sweet butter and your favorite jam. Leftover scones may be wrapped in foil and frozen for later use.

Oatmeal Lace Baskets with Strawberry Cream

It may come as a surprise to some that cookies made with oatmeal can have such an unusual texture and delicate quality about them. Indeed these cookies, which are formed into crinkly baskets to hold the strawberry cream filling, are crunchy and delicious.

The batter first is cooked on top of the stove, then baked into thin lacy circles. Please follow the instructions very carefully. Don't be put off by this — these unusual cookies are well worth the effort. With a little patience you'll soon have the knack of removing the cookies from the pan easily.

¾   cup quick cooking rolled oats (not instant)
⅓   cup butter
½   cup brown sugar, firmly packed
1   tablespoon milk
1   tablespoon all-purpose flour
1   teaspoon vanilla extract
¼   teaspoon salt

Preheat oven to 350°F. In a small saucepan melt butter. When butter is melted add the rest of the ingredients. Cook over medium heat for 3 minutes stirring constantly. Remove from heat.

Butter and flour a cookie sheet making sure that the entire surface is covered evenly. Place cooked batter on cookie sheet by teaspoonful dividing mixture into nine cookies. Allow plenty of room between cookies as they spread quite a bit while baking. You will need a muffin tin when cookies have been baked.

Place cookie sheet on center rack in oven. Bake for 8 to 10 minutes or until cookies are a golden brown. Remove pan from oven and set on cool surface. Do not try to remove the cookies from the pan yet. Allow cookies to cool for about 1 minute. Don't worry if cookies spread more than you anticipated. While they are cooling merely cut them apart with a sharp knife in places where they may have run together.

With a metal spatula gently try to remove one of the cookies from the pan by lifting carefully from the side to make sure it will hold together. If it seems to be falling apart wait another ½ minute or so before trying again. Once you are able to remove the cookies work quickly. Place each cookie on the back of a muffin cup and let cool.

Once the cookies have cooled and formed into hardened baskets you may place them in an airtight container until serving time. The filling we suggest will only be enough for two baskets but the balance of the baskets can be stored in the airtight container or frozen for future use.

Filling
8   large strawberries
¼   cup heavy cream
½   teaspoon vanilla extract
2   tablespoons confectioner's sugar

Wash strawberries and remove stems. Set aside two of the strawberries for garnish. Mash remaining strawberries. In a mixing bowl whip cream, sugar and vanilla until firm. Gently fold in the mashed strawberries. Fill two of the lace baskets. Place whole strawberry on top. Serve immediately.

You may prepare the ingredients for the filling before dinner and refrigerate until dessert time. Keep the mashed strawberries and whipped cream separate until then.

ELIZABETH BARRETT
AND
ROBERT BROWNING

How do I love thee? Let me count the ways.
I love thee to the depth and breadth and height
My soul can reach, when feeling out of sight
for the end of Being and ideal Grace.
I love thee to the level of everyday's
Most quiet need, by sun and candle-light.
I love thee freely, as men strive for Right;
I love thee purely, as they turn from Praise.
I love thee with the passion put to use
In my old griefs, and with my childhood's faith.
I love thee with a love I seemed to lose
With my lost saints, — I love thee with the breath,
Smiles, tears, of all my life! — and if God choose,
I shall but love thee better after death.

Elizabeth Barrett Browning
XLIII - Sonnets from the Portuguese

How could we describe the relationship between Elizabeth Barrett and Robert Browning without including this inspirational testimony to their love? In her own words, Elizabeth portrays the essence of her committ-ment to her husband. How wonderful he must have felt at receiving this deep expression of her love.

The experience shared by Elizabeth and Robert Browning was a rare fan-tasy in life. For each there was one and only one love, their love for each other. Among love stories in both life and fiction, theirs was a fairy tale. What makes it all the more marvelous is the fact that it was true.

Elizabeth Barrett was forty years old when she married Robert Brown-ing, six years her junior, in September of 1846. They married secretly, fearful of the influence that Elizabeth's father could have on their union, had he learned about their marriage plans. Their love had grown over a period of time, through letters and poems, until at last Robert convinced Elizabeth they could marry and be together despite her delicate health. So strong was his love that he thwarted the generally held opinion of all who knew Elizabeth at that time, that her health was too precarious for marriage. The strength of Robert's love sustained them through their secret marriage and relocation to Italy, where, beyond the reach of her father, Elizabeth blossomed as a woman and as a mother.

Shortly after their arrival in Italy, the Brownings settled more or less permanently in Florence. Although they worked separately on their poetry, much of their leisure time was spent in solemn companionship, on walks or in quiet conversation. With the change in seasons they often travelled to other parts of Italy, but they always returned to their villa in Florence. There they enjoyed the comfort of a light and airy apartment, elegantly decorated with richly carved furniture and delightful old things purchased by Robert in small shops nearby. One of the outstanding features of their quarters — and indeed, Elizabeth's link to the outer world for much of the time — was a large terrace overlooking a square, bordered on one side by the church of San Felice. It was through observations of the comings and goings of the crowds beneath her that Elizabeth developed her great love for the Italian people. Robert too developed a love for this adopted land, primarily through his interest in the politics and personalities of the day.

It is understandable that, although they lived in Italy and enjoyed the foods of that region, Elizabeth and Robert also retained a taste for the dishes found in their homes back in England. The Brownings could well afford to indulge themselves in a dinner reflecting a mixture of their English heritage and new found Italian home, while maintaining Robert's preference for a vegetarian diet.

On a warm summer's evening what better place to catch a soft cool breeze than out on the terrace. Under the stars, with the lights of Florence blinking in the background and the air heavy with the scent of newly blooming roses, Elizabeth and Robert surely would have shared an intimate dinner for two.

They might have chosen a vegetable rich minestrone, a pasta dish accompanied by a mixed salad, and a fresh fruit dessert. Our Florentine Lasagna, a dish rich in milk, cheese and fresh vegetables, captures the essence of the foods they liked. It is noteworthy that one of the herbs in this dish is Rosemary, the symbol of fidelity and remembrance. How fitting an ingredient for two single-minded lovers who found complete fulfillment in each other. The dessert, a fresh orange trifle reminiscent of English cooking, provides a contrast of textures to delight the palate.

The road between Florence and Sienna, a favorite destination for the Brownings, runs through the heart of Tuscany. This district is famous for its vineyards which produce the grapes for Chianti, a tangy wine when drunk young but one which mellows with age. The Brownings probably enjoyed this wine with many meals and it would be suitable for the one we have suggested.

Minestrone

Minestrone is commonly found on the Italian menu as a first course. In Italy the summer garden is a favorite source for fresh vegetables and aromatic herbs. Slowly simmered in this soup, they combine to reach a full-bodied flavor, enhanced by a sprinkling of Parmesan cheese.

1   small potato, peeled
1   small onion
1   stalk celery
1   medium carrot
2   plum tomatoes, peeled, seeded and chopped
½   cup cabbage
¼   cup zucchini
1   teaspoon salt
⅛   teaspoon pepper
2   tablespoons olive oil
1   teaspoon minced garlic
1   bay leaf
1   teaspoon chopped parsley
¼   teaspoon basil
3   cups water
2   tablespoons grated Parmesan cheese

Wash and peel vegetables where appropriate. Chop vegetables and place in a medium-size saucepan with olive oil. Cook over low heat until vegetables soften slightly (about 5 minutes). Add water and spices. Cover and cook for 2 hours on low heat.

Minestrone may be prepared early in the day.

Mixed Salad

Lettuce, the most common and basic component of a salad, has been eaten since early civilizations. There are many varieties of lettuce and a superb salad will have more than one kind. The controversy over when to serve the salad has existed for some time and would seem to tell us that there is no one "correct" place for it during the meal.

½   cup arugula
1   cup salad bowl lettuce or any leafy lettuce. (Ruby red
     if you can find it)
2   Italian plum tomatoes
4   hot green peppers, preferably pepperoncini
½   cup sliced zucchini
½   cup sliced carrots
2   tablespoons minced scallions

Wash lettuce under cold water and pat dry with paper towels or salad spinner. Place half of each type attractively on a plate. Wash and slice tomatoes, zucchini, and carrots. Arrange these on top of lettuce with peppers. Sprinkle with scallions. Serve with wine vinegar and olive oil.

Florentine Lasagna

This pleasing combination of cheese, spinach, and noodles is a departure from the usual tomato sauce and meat filled lasagna. It is assembled in the same manner as traditional lasagna. When finished, the top of this casserole displays a characteristic fluffy brown covering of cheese and sauce. You may prepare this lasagna early in the day and refrigerate until meal time. Or it may be prepared well in advance and frozen. If frozen it should be partially baked beforehand. Defrost and finish baking before serving.

10 ounces fresh spinach
8   ounces ricotta cheese
2   eggs
3   tablespoons butter
2   tablespoons chopped scallions
¼   cup chopped onions
1   tablespoon minced parsley
1   teaspoon rosemary
½   cup grated parmesan cheese
8   ounces mozzarella cheese
¼   teaspoon salt
⅛   teaspoon pepper
½   pound lasagna noodles, cooked al dente and drained
2   cups Béchamel sauce (page 134)
¼   cup grated parmesan cheese

Butter the bottom and sides of a 2 quart casserole. Wash spinach carefully and remove stems. Steam in top part of a double boiler (or use health steamer) until wilted. Drain and chop coarsley. Set aside.

Sauté chopped onions in butter until light brown. In a medium-size bowl, combine the steamed spinach, onions, scallions, ricotta cheese, eggs, parsley, rosemary, ½ cup parmesan cheese, ¼ teaspoon salt, and ⅛ teaspoon pepper until well blended.

To assemble: Cover bottom of buttered casserole with one layer of noodles placed side by side and cut to fit dish. Cover with ½ spinach mixture and ⅓ of Béchamel sauce. Sprinkle with ⅓ mozzarella cheese. Repeat a second layer of noodles, spinach, and mozzarella cheese. End with a layer of noodles covered with remaining ⅓ of sauce and mozzarella cheese. Sprinkle with ¼ cup grated parmesan cheese.

Bake in preheated 350°F. oven for thirty minutes or until top is brown and puffy.

Béchamel Sauce

This is a very basic white sauce which can be used in many recipes. All you need do is add ½ cup of grated cheese or substitute ½ cup white wine for ½ the milk and you have a delicious new sauce. The recipe below is meant to be used in the Florentine Lasagna*. If you want a thicker consistency, use 2 tablespoons of butter and 2 tablespoons of flour, keeping the amount of liquid the same.

    1   tablespoon butter
    1   tablespoon all-purpose flour
    1   cup milk, warmed
    ¼   teaspoon salt
    ⅛   teaspoon freshly ground pepper
    dash nutmeg (optional)

In a small saucepan, melt butter over medium heat. Add flour and stir with a wire whisk until all the flour is incorporated into the butter. Add warm milk, salt, and pepper, stirring constantly until mixture is smooth. Stir in nutmeg. Remove from heat. Makes 1 cup.

*For the Florentine Lasagna you will need two cups of sauce.

Orange Trifle

This dessert is a sumptuous blend of delicate textures. The succulence of fresh orange and the smooth sweetness of creamy custard contrast with the tangy mystery of coconut and the crispness of crushed amaretti. Prepare early in the day in order to give the various ingredients time to mingle.

4	coconut macaroons
1	tablespoon orange juice
4	teaspoons apricot brandy
1	large or two small seedless oranges, peeled and sectioned
½	cup heavy cream, whipped
1	teaspoon vanilla extract
2	teaspoons sugar
1	cup custard
4	amaretti cookies, crushed (optional)

Place macaroons in bottom of a shallow dish. Crush slightly. Moisten with brandy and orange juice. Let stand for one hour.

Cover macaroons with orange sections. Pour warm custard over oranges. Chill for 1 hour or until custard is set.

Whip cream with sugar and vanilla until able to form stiff peaks. Spread over cooled custard. Top with crushed amaretti crumbs if desired. Chill until ready to serve.

Custard

1	egg yolk
2	tablespoons sugar
½	cup heavy cream

Combine all ingredients. Cook over low heat, stirring constantly, until thickened.

CAMILLE AND ARMAND

Alexander Dumas, fils, fell in love with Madeline du Plessis, a Parisian woman of charm and beauty. Her death, before he had known her for very long, deeply affected him. In an effort to assuage his sadness he took pen and ink and eulogized his love in a drama of domestic tragedy. In 1804, inspired by genuine sorrow, he wrote *The Lady With The Camellias*, the love story of Camille Gautier and Armand Duval.

In the story the heroine, Marguerite (also known as Camille) lives a seemingly gay and carefree life in Paris as a courtesan. She is a woman of great style and ethereal beauty. Those around her do not know that her frailty is the result of an illness, consumption. Seeming to defy her sentence of death she continues to plunge herself into the whirl of Parisian society. She attends the opera and parties. Finally she meets Armand, a man unlike any she has ever known. He is a serious young lawyer from a respectable family. They fall in love instantly.

Concerned for her health he manages to convince her to leave the bustle of Paris for the countryside. There they can be alone to enjoy the serenity and each other. For some months they are surrounded by their love. Their bliss ends when Camille seems to reject Armand's love and returns to her former life in Paris.

Armand, disillusioned and embittered by what he believes is her betrayal also leaves the country house and avoids Camille for some time. Months later he finally learns the truth. His own father had convinced her that she was unworthy to associate with the Duvals. Thus she left him, sacrificing her own happiness. Finally the lovers are reunited. Armand arrives at Camille's side just in time to profess his love and beg her forgiveness before she dies.

In Paris, Marguerite was known as the lady of the Camellias. They were the only flower to grace her box at the theater. Like the flower, she was seen as a fragile, brilliant beauty. In the country Armand showered her with wild flowers which grew in abundance in the gardens around them. There Marguerite likened herself to those gay flowers, forsaking the perfection of the camellias. She was a relaxed young girl again, no longer pampered and perfectly outfitted, her love giving her new hope for the future.

Camille and Armand enjoyed being with each other and sharing simple country food. One day they might have chosen a petite version of a cassoulet, served with crisp lightly browned bread sticks and a fresh spinach salad. These could be followed by a pear tart topped with whipped cream. In the afternoon they sat and dined at a small table in the sitting room overlooking the garden. There two large windows filled with sunshine framed the lovers, illuminating their love.

Spinach Salad with Sweet and Sour Dressing

Crispy dark green leaves of spinach glisten under a tangy sweet and sour dressing. A virtual medley of vegetables, this delicious salad could be a meal in itself.

5   ounces fresh spinach
½   cup shredded green cabbage
2   tablespoons red onion, chopped
¼   cup cooked bacon, crumbled
1   hard boiled egg, chopped
3   large mushrooms, sliced

Wash spinach carefully. Drain or put in a salad spinner. Cut away hard stems. All spinach leaves should remain whole. Place spinach in a salad bowl. Sprinkle with remaining ingredients. Pour desired amount of dressing over spinach.

Dressing
⅓   cup sugar
½   cup vinegar
½   cup salad oil
1   teaspoon salt
1   clove garlic, pressed

Put all ingredients in a container. Cover tightly and shake vigorously. Store in refrigerator.

Cassoulet

This hearty bean stew is a simplified version of the classic French cassoulet. Originally it was a way for frugal housewives to use odd bits of meat and poultry. Today it qualifies as a special dinner for even the fussiest gourmet.

One can choose from many different combinations of meat and poultry when preparing a cassoulet. We have selected lamb, chicken, and a mildly spiced sausage. This results in a lighter stew, yet still retains the character of the original dish.

    1   cup white beans
    1   small onion stuck with 1 whole clove
    1-1" cube salt pork, scored
    ¼   teaspoon thyme
    1   teaspoon chopped parsley
    1   bay leaf
    2   cups chicken stock
    ½   cup dry white wine
    4   ounces Portuguese sausage, cut in ½" chunks

Put beans in a saucepan and cover with water. Bring to boil. Remove from heat and allow beans to soak for 1 ½ hours. (Or place beans in a small bowl, cover with water and soak overnight.) Before proceeding with recipe drain water from beans.

Place beans in a medium-size saucepan. Add sausage, salt pork, herbs, chicken stock, and onion. Cook over low heat for 1 ½ hours. Cook slowly to allow the flavors to blend. When necessary skim off fat from liquid. Meanwhile prepare meat.

½   pound boneless lamb, cubed
½   pound bonesless chicken, cubed
2   tablespoons butter
2   small tomatoes, peeled, seeded and chopped
1   clove garlic, chopped
1   small onion, chopped
1   small carrot, chopped
⅛   teaspoon salt
dash pepper

Topping
2   tablespoons butter, melted
¼   cup fine dry breadcrumbs
1   teaspoon parsley, chopped

Brown lamb and chicken in butter. Add chopped onion, carrot, tomatoes, garlic, salt and pepper. Cook over low heat for 10 minutes. Set aside.

When beans are cooked remove salt pork, onion, and bay leaf. Add meat mixture to beans. (May be prepared up to this point and refrigerated.) Bring mixture to simmer on top of stove before proceeding to final step.

To bake, place beans and meat in a casserole and cover with buttered bread crumbs. Bake in preheated 350°F. oven for 40 minutes. Serve immediately.

Bread Sticks

There is a special quality and texture to bread served in France. These bread sticks are similar in character, having a soft center and crisp outer crust.

> 1   teaspoon granular yeast
> ⅓   cup lukewarm water
> 2   teaspoons sugar
> 2   tablespoons butter, melted
> ½   teaspoon salt
> 1⅛   cups sifted all-purpose flour
> 1   egg, beaten

In a mixing bowl combine yeast, warm water, and sugar. Mix until yeast is completely dissolved. Allow to sit for 5 minutes.

If you are using an electric mixer set it on low while adding the rest of the ingredients. Add butter, salt, and flour mixing until they are well blended. Adjust speed to medium (change to bread hook if you have one) and beat for 3 minutes. Dough will be stiff and elastic. Place in buttered bowl, cover with damp cloth, and allow to rise until doubled in bulk (about 2 hours). Punch down and divide into six pieces. Roll between palms into 8" sticks. Place on a buttered cookie sheet leaving space between them. Brush with beaten egg. Cover and let rise for ½ hour.

Bake in preheated 325°F. oven for 20 minutes or until golden brown. Cool completely. Store in airtight bag and reheat before serving, if you like.

Pear Tart

It seems certain that pears were known to early Greek civilizations, if not before then. In France, beginning in the latter part of the eighteenth century, great efforts were made to produce new and better quality pears. As a result of these efforts, as well as those in places like Italy, Holland, and the United States, there are hundreds of varieties of pears today. Each one is uniquely appreciated for its difference in size, shape, texture, and flavor. We suggest using fresh Bartlett pears which have a green skin and boast a firm white flesh. Three-quarters of the pears grown in America are Bartlett and so they can easily be found.

½   cup sweet butter
½   cup all-purpose flour
2   tablespoons sugar
1   tablespoon cold water
pinch salt
2   ripe pears
¼   cup apple jelly
¼   cup heavy cream
1   teaspoon sugar

With a pastry blender, combine butter, flour, sugar, water, and salt until they form a ball of dough. Pat dough into a greased 8-inch fluted tart pan with floured fingertips.

Peel pears, remove seeds and center stem. Slice into pieces about ½" thick. Arrange in pin wheel fashion over crust. Bake in preheated 400°F. oven for 35 minutes. Cool on wire rack.

When tart is cooled, heat jelly until it liquifies. Spread over top of baked tart. Whip cream and sugar. Serve separately.

SCARLETT O'HARA
AND
RHETT BUTLER

When Margaret Mitchell wrote *Gone With The Wind* and created the characters of Scarlett O'Hara and Rhett Butler, could she ever have guessed that these two flamboyant lovers would become part of American culture? Scarlett O'Hara is eternally the spirited and willfully selfish southern belle with the tenacity to survive against enormous odds. Rhett Butler always will be that dear and glorious rascal who loved her, and waited for her to realize that she loved him too.

The spirit and the fire of these two larger than life characters sparks a blaze to rival the burning of Atlanta. For over a thousand pages they jest. They battle. They kiss. And they suffer with unforgettable passion.

For an intimate dinner for two, we find them on their honeymoon in New Orleans, a calm interlude in their otherwise tempestuous relationship. Here alone together for a few brief, halcyon days, they are free from the shadows of the past and blissfully unaware of the pain the future holds.

The inspiration for this sinfully rich dinner is taken from the actual list of foods mentioned in Margaret Mitchell's creation of their honeymoon week. Scarlett, unfettered by inhibition or poverty as the new Mrs. Butler, accompanies her husband on a whirlwind trip to this exciting city. Gone are the ghosts of the war years. For a time they forget the horror of the destruction of Atlanta and the privation of Scarlett's years at Tara. With hedonistic abandon they revel in the bustling, raucous, fun-filled city, full of laughter, music, and champagne.

We begin our meal with a tasty oyster dish which reflects the popularity of this delicacy in New Orleans. It is followed by a savory shrimp course, redolent with the heady spices of Louisiana Creole cookery. Finally, the

rich chocolate mousse pie is laced with bourbon and, in a wonderfully extravagant gesture, is topped with bourbon-flavored whipped cream.
Throughout the meal Scarlett and Rhett toast each other with cold sparkl-
ing champagne, the wine which has become the traditional drink for
special occasions.

Devilish Oysters

Oysters always have been considered a delicacy. They can be prepared in many ways. We have chosen to present them chopped and seasoned to perfection and baked in individual ramekins.

6   fresh oysters, chopped
1   tablespoon butter
1   tablespoon chopped scallions
¼   cup chopped mushrooms
¼   teaspoon dry mustard
dash Worcestershire sauce
¼   teaspoon chopped parsley
pinch cayenne pepper
½   cup cracker crumbs (Ritz type)
2   tablespoons grated cheddar cheese

In a small frying pan over medium heat, sauté scallions and mushrooms until soft. Add oysters, mustard, Worcestershire sauce, parsley, and pepper. Cook until the oysters are firm. Remove from heat and add cracker crumbs. Mix well.

Butter two small ramekins. Divide mixture in half and spoon into ramekins. Top each with 1 tablespoon grated cheddar cheese. (May be prepared up to this point and refrigerated.) Before serving bake at 375°F. for 15 minutes.

Shrimp à la Creole

Creole cooking is native to Louisiana and its environs, having been brought there by Spanish and French settlers. The Spanish are responsible for the liberal use of spices; the French for the addition of wine. Our use of cream further enhances this otherwise traditional creole recipe.

> 1   *tablespoon butter*
> 1   *tablespoon minced onion*
> 1   *tablespoon minced celery*
> 1   *tablespoon all-purpose flour*
> 1   *teaspoon chopped parsley*
> ⅛   *teaspoon salt*
> *dash white pepper*
> 2   *dashes Tabasco sauce*
> ½   *pound shrimp, shelled and cleaned*
> ½   *cup heavy cream*
> ½   *cup dry white wine*
> 1   *cup stewed tomatoes, coarsely chopped*
> ¼   *cup liquid from the tomatoes*

Sauté onions and celery in butter over medium heat until softened. Add flour and stir until well blended. Stir in cream, wine, tomatoes, and the tomato liquid until sauce is smooth. Add parsley, salt, pepper, and Tabasco. (May be prepared up to this point early in the day and refrigerated.)

   Just before serving, heat sauce over low heat. Add raw shrimp and cook 5 to 7 minutes or until shrimp turn pink.

To complement the shrimp creole we suggest plain boiled rice with a little butter.

> ½   *cup long grain white rice*
> 1 ¼ *cups water*
> ½   *teaspoon salt*
> 1   *tablespoon butter*

In a small covered saucepan, bring water, salt, and butter to boil. Add rice and stir. Cover and cook over very low heat for 15 to 20 minutes until all the water is absorbed. Flake with a fork.

Green Beans With Mushrooms

Buttered green beans are a classic vegetable. They are most delicious when quick cooked and still crisp.

½   *pound fresh green beans*
¼   *cup mushrooms, sliced*
1   *tablespoon butter*
¼   *teaspoon salt*

Wash green beans and slice lengthwise. Drop beans into 1″ of rapidly boiling salted water. Cook for 10 minutes. Test for doneness. Beans should still retain a hint of crunchiness.

Meanwhile, in a separate pan, sauté mushrooms in butter. When beans are done drain well and add to mushrooms. Toss well and serve.

Beans may be boiled ahead of time. To keep them green plunge them into cold water after boiling and then drain. Set aside until ready to toss with butter and mushrooms.

Chocolate Mousse Pie

As befits a dish from New Orleans, this dessert has its origins in the classic cuisine of France. Add the Southern accents of bourbon and pecans and one produces a dessert that is a veritable melange of textures and flavors. The nutty crushed pecan crust is filled with the dark brown velvet mousse and whipped cream spiked with bourbon. Certainly it is a concoction worthy of these celebrated lovers and your own very special dinner. Plan to make the pie early in the day or the day before serving, as it must be well chilled to hold its shape.

Pecan Crust
1 ½ cups pecans, finely chopped
3   tablespoons sugar
4   tablespoons butter, melted

Combine ingredients until well blended. Press into an 8-inch pie plate. Bake at 375°F. for 8 minutes. Cool and chill until ready to fill.

Chocolate Mousse
2   one ounce squares unsweetened chocolate
2   one ounce squares semi-sweet chocolate
1   ounce bourbon whiskey
1   ounce water
4   eggs, separated
½   cup superfine sugar
dash salt

Place chocolate, bourbon, and water in the top of a double boiler over simmering water. Stir once or twice when the chocolate begins to melt. Then let chocolate melt slowly while you continue with the recipe. Allow to cool.

Separate eggs. Place the yolks in a bowl with the sugar and beat until mixture is fluffy and very pale yellow. Beat egg whites with a dash of salt in a separate bowl until stiff but not dry.

Stir cooled melted chocolate into egg yolks. Combine chocolate mixture and beaten egg whites by first stirring ¼ of egg whites into chocolate. Then carefully fold in remaining egg whites. Pour into prepared pie shell and chill until serving time.

Just before serving decorate top of pie with six dollops of whipped cream. Remaining whipped cream may be passed in a small bowl.

Whipped Cream

½   pint heavy cream
2   tablespoons superfine sugar
1   tablespoon bourbon whiskey
             or
1   teaspoon vanilla extract

Beat all ingredients in a chilled bowl until firm peaks may be formed. Spoon onto pie.

RICHARD WAGNER
AND
COSIMA LIZST

In their villa, beneath the jagged Swiss mountain peaks and overlooking the placid water of Lake Lucerne, Richard Wagner and Cosima Lizst lived only for each other. Both had been previously married and their courtship was fraught with public scandal. But their devotion to each other gave them the strength to defy contemporary mores in order to be together.

Cosima, the daughter of the composer Franz Lizst, was twenty years younger than Richard. Although delicate and slender in appearance her strong facial features hinted at a forceful character within. When they first met Cosima seemed to be in awe of the great musician. However, as she accepted his genius, she proceeded to devote herself to its continued development. In many ways she brought order to his otherwise tempestuous life. She was his helpmate, his ambassador of good will. Her sense of humor delighted him, as did her continuous support and efforts to surround them with gaiety.

For Richard the years in Switzerland were among the happiest in his life. Although he had a tremendous amount of talent and was unceasingly devoted to his music, there always seemed to be some financial problem plaguing him. In truth, Wagner had to depend often on the good will and generosity of his friends for many of life's necessities. At last he had found some peace from the pressures of the previous years. Now he could devote himself to the development of his unique style of music.

Wagner's music wove a potent spell around audiences throughout Europe. Grounded in the realm of myths and fairy tales, his works had a romanticism all their own. Their dramatic, compelling force brought a new dimension to the world of opera in the late 1870's.

The sheer beauty of Switzerland's rolling hills and deep fertile valleys was ideal for Wagner's concentration. There, among the small picturesque farms, he could devote himself to his music. Although their house was often crowded with visitors we like to think that our lovers would have taken time to be alone. On one such morning in their Villa Triebschen, sitting tall on the crest of a hill overlooking the lake, Cosima and Richard might hear the clang of cow bells off in the distance. They would be reminded of the excellent dairy products made on those farms and think about how very much they enjoyed Swiss cooking. For breakfast, they might choose an apple pancake, rich with fresh milk and eggs. On the side might be ground sausage patties flavored with sage. To accompany the pancakes and sausage patties we suggest chocolate flavored Swiss coffee and a struesel topped coffee cake.

Apple Pancake

Pancakes come in many varieties. Sometimes flour is used as a base. Other choices range from cornmeal and cornstarch to potatoes and other vegetables. Pancakes, thin or thick, may be stacked, rolled, or filled. This apple pancake is baked in the oven with the fruit already on top. Beaten egg whites give it a light, puffy consistency.

Apples
2   large Cortland apples
2   tablespoons butter
2   tablespoons light brown sugar
¼   teaspoon ground cinnamon

Batter
5   eggs, separated
¼   cup all-purpose flour
¼   cup sugar
¼   cup milk
½   teaspoon vanilla extract

Topping
6   teaspoons sugar
½   teaspoon ground cinnamon

Preheat oven to 400°F. Peel and core apples. Cut into ½ inch pieces. In a medium-size frying pan, melt 2 tablespoons butter. Add brown sugar, cinnamon, and apples. Cook over low heat for 10 minutes.

Beat egg whites until stiff. In a separate bowl, beat egg yolks, flour, sugar, milk, and vanilla until smooth. Fold in beaten egg whites.

Have 2 9-inch baking pans ready. Place 2 tablespoons butter in each pan. Melt in oven but be careful that the butter doesn't burn. Turn pan so that butter covers entire bottom surface. Fill each pan with ½ of the batter. Distribute apples on top of each pancake. Top with cinnamon and sugar.

Bake at 400°F. for 10 minutes. Loosen sides and bottom with metal spatula. Serve immediately with maple syrup.

Sausage Patties

Sausages are an essential part of the German-Swiss culinary heritage. They come in many different sizes and shapes and can be fresh, cooked, or dried. These small golden brown patties are flavored with sage and should be served hot.

    6   ounces ground breakfast sausage
    1   tablespoon bread crumbs
    ¼   teaspoon sage
    1   teaspoon butter

Combine sausage meat, bread crumbs and sage until well blended. The sausage mixture may be prepared early in the day and stored in the refrigerator until brunch.

Melt 1 teaspoon butter in a frying pan. Form meat into 4 patties. Brown meat thoroughly on both sides over medium heat.

Sour Cream Coffee Cake

Sour cream is a key ingredient in this streusel filled coffee cake. Light and crumbly in texture it is topped with a thin sugar glaze.

¼ cup sweet butter (½ stick)
¼ cup granulated sugar
¼ cup light brown sugar, firmly packed
1 egg
½ teaspoon vanilla extract
1 cup sifted all-purpose flour
½ teaspoon baking powder
½ teaspoon baking soda
¼ teaspoon salt
½ cup sour cream

Topping
1 tablespoon sweet butter, melted
¼ cup light brown sugar, firmly packed
1 tablespoon all-purpose flour
1 teaspoon ground cinnamon
¼ cup walnuts, chopped
¼ cup raisins
dash nutmeg

In a small bowl stir topping ingredients together. Set aside.

Cream butter and sugars in bowl of electric mixer. Add egg and vanilla and mix well. Sift flour, baking powder, baking soda, and salt together. Add to butter, alternating with sour cream. Beat until batter is smooth.

Grease and flour an 8-inch springform pan. Put ½ the batter in the pan. Cover with ½ the topping. Repeat ending with topping.

Bake in preheated 350°F. oven for 40 minutes or until a toothpick inserted in center comes out clean. Cool on wire rack.

When cake has cooled prepare sugar glaze.

Glaze
½   cup confectioners' sugar
2   teaspoons milk
¼   teaspoon vanilla extract

Beat sugar, milk, and vanilla until very smooth and mixture begins to thicken. Remove sides of cake pan. Spoon glaze over cooled cake allowing it to drip over sides. Top with a bright red cherry.

Swiss Mocha Coffee

Switzerland is world famous for its chocolate. This drink will be richly flavored by a Swiss cocoa and strong coffee.

2   cups strong black coffee
2   cups hot cocoa, made with milk
¼   cup heavy cream, whipped

Combine hot coffee and hot cocoa in one pot. Keep warm until serving time. Pour into cups and top with whipped cream.

DIAMOND JIM BRADY
AND
LILLIAN RUSSELL

Of all the famous pairs in this book perhaps none enjoyed food more than Diamond Jim Brady and Lillian Russell. At the height of their success extravagance was the essence of their life style. Diamond Jim was a self-made man. A resident of New York's rough and tumble Hell's Kitchen, he rose in a surprisingly short time to one of the flashiest, wealthiest men of his time. His meteoric rise to supersalesman was due to a combination of imaginative thinking, hard work, a convivial personality, and some luck.

Lillian Russell (nee Helen Louise Leonard), first publicized as an English ballad singer, was in reality a small town girl from Iowa. As a young starlet, Lillian's beauty reached out over the footlights with a kind of sexual magnetism. Blond and slim, she provoked many male members of her audience to shower her with unexpected flowers and lavish gifts. Largely because of her career and the wealth it brought she was able to indulge in an unconventional life-style.

Although they had met several times before, Jim and Lillian first began seeing each other regularly at the Columbian Exposition of 1893 in Chicago. Their love of and great capacity for food provided the basis for the friendship that blossomed between them.

Thrust to the forefront of a period known for its gaiety and extravagance, Diamond Jim and Lillian played their parts well. They eagerly sought out each other's company, to gorge themselves in sheer decadence on the richest, most expensive foods available. Dinner usually consisted of several courses and lasted far into the night. Lobster, steak, chocolate confections. . . nothing was too costly or too lavish.

Our scaled down version of a gay nineties' dinner highlights some of

Jim's and Lillian's favorite dishes. After the theater they arrive at one of New York's most posh restaurants. Seated beneath crystal chandeliers and surrounded by tapestried walls, the strains of a rag time band in the background, our famous couple dine in baronial splendor. They start with individual portions of Lobster Americaine, lobster simmered in wine, tomatoes and herbs. This is followed by small rounds of beef, pan broiled and bathed in a delicately seasoned wine sauce. Delmonico potatoes, first introduced in New York's famed Delmonico's Restaurant, and fresh asparagus with Hollandaise sauce complete this ostentatious course. For dessert our couple would choose something sweet and rich, followed by hand dipped chocolates. We have devised a chocolate cherry bon bon cake which is reminiscent of a candy like confection.

When you want to celebrate your own success, follow Diamond Jim's and Lillian's credo and prepare this lavish dinner for two.

Lobster Americaine

This most expensive of shellfish is a fitting first course for Diamond Jim and Lillian. Its extravagance matches the spirit of the age in which they lived. New York in the 1890's was famous for its "Lobster Palaces," restaurants which catered to the tastes of the new breed of millionaires. When he didn't begin his meal with several dozen oysters, Diamond Jim often chose this rich aromatic dish of lobster, wine, tomatoes, and herbs.

6	ounces cooked lobster meat
2	tablespoons olive oil
2	tablespoons finely chopped shallots
¼	clove garlic, finely minced
1	teaspoon tarragon
1	teaspoon parsley
3	Italian plum tomatoes, peeled, seeded and chopped
2	tablespoons brandy
¼	cup white wine
⅛	teaspoon salt
	dash cayenne pepper
1	tablespoon butter + ¼ cup bread crumbs for topping

Coarsely chop lobster meat keeping two whole claws for garnish, if possible. In a medium-size frying pan, sauté shallots in olive oil until limp and transparent. Add chopped tomatoes, garlic, tarragon, and parsley. Cook for 2 to 3 minutes. Meanwhile warm brandy in a small saucepan.

Add lobster to herb mixture being careful not to break the two whole claws. Stir briefly. Then pour the warm brandy over lobster mixture and flame immediately. When flame dies down, add white wine. Simmer for 5 minutes. Remove whole claws. Add butter, salt, and pepper. Allow ingredients to simmer until butter has melted.

Spoon mixture into two scallop shells or small ramekins. Melt 1 tablespoon butter; add bread crumbs and mix well. Spoon half the crumbs on each shell and top with whole claw. (May be prepared up to this point and then refrigerated.) Allow to come to room temperature before baking.

Preheat oven to 350°F. Bake lobster for 10 minutes to heat thoroughly.

Filet Mignon

The best steak requires very little attention. Filet mignon is one of the most expensive steaks you can buy. Panfrying seals in the juices and careful timing insures that the meat will be tender.

> 2   *1" thick filet mignon steaks (approximately 8 ounces each)*
> ¼   *teaspoon salt*
> ⅛   *teaspoon pepper*
> 3   *tablespoons butter*
> ¼   *cup Burgundy wine*

Rub salt and pepper on both sides of steak. Melt 1 tablespoon butter in a medium-size frying pan over medium-high heat. Brown steak on both sides. Lower heat and cook to desired degree of doneness.

    Rare: 4 minutes per side

    Medium: 5 minutes per side

    Well done: 7 minutes per side

  To test for doneness, use a very sharp knife to make a slit in the center of the steak. Transfer steaks to warm plates.

  Turn heat to medium. Deglaze pan with ¼ cup wine. Be sure to scrape up any browned bits of meat left in the pan. Add 2 tablespoons butter and stir until the butter melts. Pour sauce over steaks and serve.

Asparagus with Hollandaise Sauce

The railroad, the key to Diamond Jim's wealth, made possible the distribution of the tremendous array of foodstuffs available in the late 1800's. Such was the case with regionally grown vegetables. Tender young shoots of asparagus always have been treasured as a luxury vegetable. In the gay nineties it often was featured on the menus of expensive restaurants.

1   *pound fresh asparagus*

Wash asparagus and cut off lower part of stalks. Place in a 2 quart saucepan. Add 1 cup boiling water, cover and gently steam for 12 minutes or until tender. Drain well and serve with hollandaise.

Sauce
2   *egg yolks*
½   *teaspoon salt*
dash cayenne pepper
½   *cup butter, melted*
1   *tablespoon lemon juice*

Using electric mixer or blender, beat egg yolks until thick. Add salt and pepper. Add 3 tablespoons of the melted butter a little at a time, beating constantly.
   Then slowly pour in rest of butter alternating with lemon juice until mixture is smooth and well blended. May be kept warm over hot (not boiling) water.

Delmonico Potatoes

Delmonico's restaurant became famous for many of its creative dishes. One, still very popular, is Delmonico potatoes; potatoes in a rich cheese sauce — a marvelous accompaniment to a filet mignon.

2   *small potatoes*
1   *cup thin Béchamel Sauce (page 134)*
½   *cup grated medium sharp cheddar cheese*
⅛   *teaspoon salt*
pinch pepper
½   *tablespoon butter, melted*
2   *tablespoons bread crumbs*

Peel, boil and dice potatoes. Combine with Béchamel Sauce, salt and pepper.

Butter a small casserole. Layer potato mixture and cheese. Top with bread crumbs mixed with butter.

Bake at 375°F. for 20 minutes.

Chocolate Cherry Bon Bon Cake

This luscious dessert is meant to resemble a large chocolate bon bon, one of the sweets our famous pair adored. It is baked in a bowl, then cut into three layers, which are spread with cherry jam and whipped cream flavored with Kirsch.

½ cup sugar
3 eggs, separated
2 tablespoons all-purpose flour
1 ounce unsweetened chocolate, melted and cooled

Preheat oven to 350°F. Line a medium-size stainless steel bowl with aluminum foil and butter well.

Cream sugar, egg yolks, and flour. Add melted chocolate and blend well. Beat egg whites until stiff but not dry. Stir ⅓ of egg whites into chocolate mixture to lighten it. Then gently fold remaining egg whites into batter. Pour into prepared bowl and bake for 25 to 30 minutes until a toothpick inserted in the center comes out clean.

Allow to cool for five minutes before inverting on a cooling rack. Carefully peel off foil and cool completely.

Filling
½ cup heavy cream
2 teaspoons Kirsch
¼ cup cherry jam

Chocolate glaze
3 tablespoons sweet butter
½ cup semi-sweet chocolate bits

Whip cream with sugar until stiff. Fold in 1 teaspoon Kirsch.

Blend jam and remaining teaspoon Kirsch.

Carefully cut cake into three even layers. Place the largest one on a serving plate. Brush with ½ of the jam and spoon on ½ of the whipped cream. Repeat for second layer. End with layer of cake.

Prepare glaze. Melt butter and chocolate. Blend until smooth. Pour over entire surface of cake. When chocolate has cooled and hardened you may refrigerate until serving time.

LARA
AND
ZHIVAGO

The love story of Yurii Zhivago and Lara Antipov is revealed eloquently in Boris Pasternak's sweeping Russian novel, *Doctor Zhivago*. From the teeming city of Moscow to the frozen waste lands of Siberia the two lovers were caught up in a storm of passion, despair, and hope. The chaos of early twentieth century Russia was a powerful force to contend with, but Lara and Yurii still were able to create a haven from the world around them, if only for a brief time.

What manner of man is Yurii Zhivago? He is a young doctor, a silent rebel who wishes only to survive in an ordinary way. He is sensitive and an intellectual in an age that no longer needs or wants these virtues. Here is a man who wants only to live in peace but is trapped in a country torn apart by revolution and civil war. In the end he is a man alone. But during the tumultuous years of the revolution he finds solace in a dream. His dream, Lara . . . a beautiful woman he encounters for fleetingly short moments.

And what of Lara? Is she just a dream? For Yurii she might be. She is drawn to him despite the opposing forces in their lives. Not only is she beautiful but she possesses a beauty in spirit as well. Life is difficult for her but she emerges from her trials still endowed with a purity and simple honesty. Ultimately, she comes to love Yurii with an unquestioning passion. For a short time they revel in the joy of love and the happiness of discovering each other.

All around them the war ravages the vastness that is Russia. The Romanov's, the ruling family, are toppled from power. Neighbor fights neighbor. Bolsheviks murder Socialists and a way of life is changed forever. What emerged was a new order, a new ideology which has made Russia one of the most powerful countries in the world.

When we think of Russia we think of a country whose size is immense. Her people are made up of many different nationalities, each possessing a unique language, tradition, and cuisine. For many of the people in the early twentieth century food was hard to come by. What was available was prepared simply. During the time in which this story is set it would have been almost impossible to dine on anything as elaborate as the dinner we suggest, but let us imagine for now that Lara and Yurii are free to savor the foods of a more peaceful age.

Their meal reflects the rich, robust nature of Russian cooking, a cuisine which has emerged from the varied cultures and people within its borders. Herring salad makes an appropriate first course and should be served with thin slices of Russian black bread. The classic Beef Stroganoff was created for a Russian Count in the late nineteenth century. What better dessert than blintzes, thin pancakes filled with sweetened cheese and smothered in blueberries and sour cream. This is truly a Russian dinner, honoring a man and woman who fell in love, in spite of the chaos that surrounded them.

Herring Salad

Herring is often part of a first course or "zakuska" in Russia. There unprocessed herring fillets may easily be purchased and adapted to recipes at home. Unfortunately, in this country the most readily available herring comes in jars and is already flavored. Still it is possible to use these fillets for this fancy herring salad.

6   *ounces pickled herring fillets (boneless, in clear liquid)*
1   *medium potato*
1   *small stalk celery, diced*
½   *cup cubed pickled beets*
1   *hard boiled egg, chopped*
1   *medium apple, peeled and diced*
1   *tablespoon sour cream*
1   *tablespoon mayonnaise*
1   *teaspoon sugar*
     dash pepper

Boil potato until it is soft but not mushy. Rinse in cold water.

If herring is from a jar be sure to drain. Then pick over to be sure there are no bones. Cut fillets into ½" pieces.

Place herring in a medium-size bowl. Peel potato and cut into ½" pieces. Add potato, celery, beets, egg, and apple to herring.

In a separate bowl combine sour cream, mayonnaise, lemon juice, sugar, and pepper. Pour over herring and stir gently until all ingredients are well coated. Cover and store in refrigerator until serving time.

Beef Stroganoff

Russian food is well known for its robust quality. Beef often is chosen for the main course. Sour cream and mushrooms are popular ingredients also. Use a good quality steak which can be cooked quickly.

1   *pound sirloin or tenderloin steak*
2   *heaping tablespoons chopped onion*
2   *tablespoons butter*
¼   *pound mushrooms, sliced*
¼   *teaspoon salt*
⅛   *teaspoon pepper*
½   *teaspoon Dijon style mustard*
½   *cup sour cream*
¼   *cup pale dry sherry*
dash nutmeg
½   *teaspoon prepared white horseradish*

In medium-size saucepan, sauté onion in 1 tablespoon butter. Add beef and cook over medium heat for 5 minutes. Remove meat and set aside.

Add 1 tablespoon of butter to same pan and sauté mushrooms for 2 to 3 minutes. Add seasonings and sherry. Cook until mixture bubbles. Add sour cream and meat. Stir and heat through making sure mixture does not boil.

Caraway Noodles

Noodles are popular in many countries. Egg noodles are an especially nice complement to Beef Stroganoff. The flavor of caraway seeds give these a unique taste.

4   *ounces egg noodles*
2   *tablespoons butter, melted*
¼   *teaspoon salt*
pinch pepper
½   *teaspoon caraway seeds*

Cook noodles in boiling salted water until tender. Drain. Toss with melted butter, salt, pepper, and caraway seeds.

Blini with Blueberry Sauce

Blini, the traditional Russian pancakes, are usually served as an appetizer with caviar and sour cream. Over the years they also have emerged as a popular dessert. When filled with cheese and served with a fruit sauce as they are here, they are more commonly known as blintzes.

Pancakes *(makes 6)*
½   cup sifted all-purpose flour
¼   teaspoon salt
⅓   cup cold water
1   egg
¼   cup milk
1   tablespoon sugar
3   tablespoons sweet butter, melted

Filling
½   cup farmer's cheese
1   egg yolk
2   tablespoons sugar

Whisk all ingredients, except butter, until smooth. Let sit for 10 minutes before cooking. Place a 6-inch frying pan or crêpe pan over medium-high heat. Heat until a drop of water skids across pan. Brush the hot pan lightly with melted butter. Pour ¼ cup of batter in pan. Grasping handle, turn pan quickly so that batter spreads over entire bottom surface. Let cook for about 2 minutes until the underside is a light brown. Flip the finished pancake onto a plate and continue until all the batter is used up. You do not need to turn the pancake over because the other side will cook after the blini is filled. Pancakes may be stacked.

Mix filling ingredients together until blended. To assemble blini, place one cooked-side up in front of you. Spoon ⅙ of the filling in the center. Fold so that the edges are turned under. Filled pancakes can be stored in the refrigerator.

Just before serving melt 1 tablespoon of butter in a medium-size frying pan. Place blini folded side down and brown. Turn and brown on other side. Serve immediately with Blueberry Sour Cream Sauce.

Blueberry Sour Cream Sauce
¾   cup fresh or frozen blueberries
½   cup sour cream
1   tablespoon sugar
⅛   teaspoon lemon rind, grated

Combine sour cream, sugar, and lemon rind. Gently fold in blueberries. Serve cold.

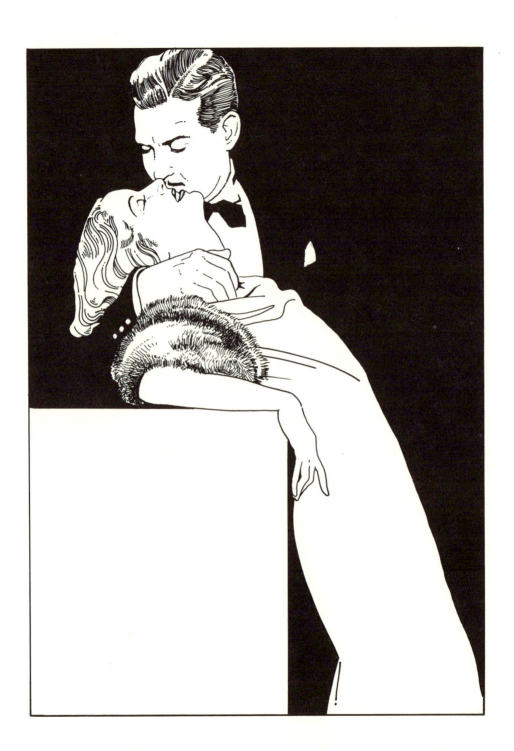

CLARK GABLE
AND
CAROLE LOMBARD

He was the King of Hollywood and she was his Queen. In the glittery world of celluloid gods and goddesses, they were the royal couple. Clark Gable was the ruggedly handsome "he-man" with a charisma that made women swoon and fantasize. Carole Lombard, a coolly beautiful, elegant blonde, with a penchant for practical jokes and salty language, was his adoring wife.

Old movie stills capture them as the quintessence of thirties' chic, slim and sophisticated, poised forever in white tie and tails and long bias-cut satin gown. But there was another side to their life together. Snapshots from the family album show them fishing, hunting, horseback riding, and clowning together. Perhaps it was this diversity that made them stand out among the fabulous array of movie stars of that era. Their life was a blending of two worlds, reality and make believe, and the linking of their names still evokes the memory of their love story.

They met in 1932 while filming the romantic comedy called *No Man of Her Own*. The stars acted and laughed together but apparently did not fall in love then. When they had finished filming (according to Hollywood folklore), Clark's leading lady presented him with a very large ham. Following that first of many practical jokes, they went back to their separate lives until three years later, when romance bloomed between them.

They purchased a hideaway that would be for them their retreat from the frenzy of movie land. On this twenty acre ranch in Encino, California, lush with flowers and fruit trees, they began their married life. He called her "Ma" and she called him "Pa." The few years they had together were filled with laughter and love.

Their evenings together were precious to them. No matter how casual or harried the day's activities had been, dinner usually was served formally in the ranch's spacious dining room. Carole set the large, highly polished table with her fine English china and antique silverware. The carefully decorated room had pine panelled walls, a beamed ceiling, oak floors, and colonial furnishings which gave the room the aura of an early American tavern.

After a long day on the set, Clark and Carole could unwind with cocktails and cheese sticks before enjoying one of the down-home meals Clark loved. Their cook, Jessie, busy in the kitchen, has prepared some of his all-American favorites. The chicken and herbed dumplings are especially tender and flavorful after being slowly simmered. Tonight's vegetable is a butternut squash spiced with ginger. As a special surprise, dessert is a Devil's food cake with homemade vanilla ice cream topped with a caramel-brandy sauce.

Cheese Sticks

Melt-in-your-mouth bits of cheddar shortbread are an excellent companion to a before dinner drink. This rich but simple finger food can be prepared ahead and baked just before serving.

6   tablespoons butter
3   ounces cheddar cheese, grated
1   cup all-purpose flour
dash cayenne pepper
¼   teaspoon salt
1   teaspoon poppy seeds

Combine all ingredients and mix well. Form into a ball, wrap and chill.

To bake preheat oven to 400°F. Divide dough into 24 pieces. Roll between fingers into 3-inch sticks. Place on ungreased cookie sheet. Bake for 12 minutes or until lightly browned.

Savory Chicken with Herbed Dumplings

Ah! the versatile chicken. It can be baked, broiled, fried, roasted, or simmered in an old fashioned stew. Rich with aromatic herbs and vegetables this recipe produces a tender, well flavored meat in a satiny sauce. Small herbed dumplings crown this savory dish.

2½ - 3	*pound chicken, cut into 8 pieces or two large whole chicken breasts, deboned*
2	*tablespoons butter*
3	*cups water*
1	*small carrot*
1	*celery stalk with top*
1	*small whole onion*
1	*tablespoon parsley*
1	*tablespoon chopped chives*
1	*teaspoon rosemary leaves, crushed*
1	*teaspoon salt*
⅛	*teaspoon pepper*

In a large pot, brown chicken in 2 tablespoons of butter. Add water, carrot, celery, onion, parsley, rosemary, chives, salt, and pepper. Cook, uncovered, 45 minutes over low heat. Remove chicken and set aside. Discard vegetables and reserve stock. Prepare sauce.

Sauce

3	*tablespoons all-purpose flour*
3	*tablespoons butter*
	chicken stock
	milk
	salt
	pepper

In a medium-size saucepan, melt butter and flour over medium heat. Stir with a wire whisk until all the flour has been incorporated into the butter. Measure stock and add enough milk to make 4 cups of liquid. Add this slowly into the pan and whisk until it is smooth. Cook over low heat until sauce has thickened. Add salt and pepper to taste.

Return chicken to pot. (May be prepared up to this point a day ahead and refrigerate.) Before adding dumplings heat chicken to boiling point.

Dumplings
1   cup sifted all-purpose flour
2   teaspoons baking powder
½   teaspoon salt
2   tablespoons vegetable oil
½   cup milk
1   tablespoon parsley
⅛   teaspoon rosemary
⅛   teaspoon onion powder

Sift together dry ingredients plus seasonings in a medium bowl. Add oil and milk. Mix lightly with a fork until blended.

Drop batter by tablespoonsful onto boiling chicken. Reduce heat and simmer, uncovered, for 10 minutes. Cover and simmer 10 minutes longer. Serve immediately.

Gingered Squash

Squash is a truly American vegetable. Of the many varieties available, we chose butternut for its flavor and bright orange color.

1   *small butternut squash*
3   *tablespoons butter*
1   *tablespoon brown sugar*
½   *teaspoon powdered ginger*
dash nutmeg

Peel, core and cut squash into 1-inch cubes. Simmer in a small amount of water or steam until squash is easily pierced with a fork. Drain well and mash with remaining ingredients. Place in a small buttered casserole and set aside. Before serving bake in a preheated 325°F. oven for 20 minutes.

Devil's Food Pound Cake

Originally the pound cake was so named because it contained a pound each of its basic ingredients: sugar, butter, eggs, and flour. Today the proportions have changed; however, the basic texture remains the same.

This dense Devil's food pound cake combines the texture of one American favorite with the flavor of another.

Cake
1   stick sweet butter (½ cup)
¼   cup brown sugar, firmly packed
¼   cup granulated sugar
2   squares unsweetened chocolate, melted and cooled
3   eggs at room temperature
dash cloves
¼   teaspoon ground cinnamon
½   teaspoon vanilla extract
¼   teaspoon salt
1   cup sifted all-purpose flour
¼   teaspoon baking powder

Caramel Sauce
½   cup sugar
½   cup boiling water
2   tablespoons brandy

Preheat oven to 300°F. Grease and flour an 8-inch loaf pan.

Cream butter and sugar. Add vanilla and eggs one at a time. Beat until smooth. Add melted chocolate. Beat again until all of the chocolate is incorporated into the batter.

Sift together flour, baking powder, salt, and spices. Add to chocolate mixture. Beat 2 minutes at medium speed of an electric mixer or 400 strokes by hand.

Pour into prepared pan. Tilt batter up sides and into corners for even baking. Bake at 300°F. for 50 minutes or until a cake tester inserted into center of cake comes out clean. Cool in pan on wire rack for 10 minutes. Then remove cake from pan and cool on rack.

Meanwhile, prepare sauce. In a small saucepan, heat sugar overlow heat until it melts and is slightly brown. Stir constantly. Then slowly add boiling water. Cook approximately 5 minutes. Cool slightly. Add brandy. Store in glass jar in refrigerator.

To assemble dessert, place slice of cake on serving plate. Spoon 1 tablespoon caramel sauce over cake. Add 1 scoop ice cream and cover with 2 to 3 more tablespoons of sauce.

RICK
AND
ILSA

You must remember this
A kiss is just a kiss
A sigh is just a sigh
The world will always welcome lovers
As time goes by

"Play it again Sam. If you can play it for her, you can play it for me." Who can ever forget those words or that song once they have seen the film "Casablanca"? Humphrey Bogart and Ingrid Bergman, in the roles of Rick and Ilsa, are among the screen's most famous lovers. Theirs was a moment in time, a short interlude of love which gained importance for each as a memory. It was a special time which could not be recaptured but would never be forgotten.

The lovers met in Paris, city of love, the week before the German army swept brazenly through a bitterly defeated populace. Richard Blaine, a soldier of fortune, maintained his neutrality in the explosive political situation around him. By chance he met Ilsa Laslo, a beautiful, mysterious woman with whom he immediately fell in love. Blind to the past and the future, they grasped the present until relentlessly beset by the outside world. Then, torn by the horrors of war and a web of personal complications they were separated, their destinies propelled in different directions.

Years later, in Rick's saloon in Casablanca, they are reunited. Their love and memories, painfully remembered, are sparked into life by the words and music of a song (*As Time Goes By*), the symbol of their never forgotten passion.

Fleetingly they cannot help but turn their thoughts to the possibility of a reconciliation. At last, the haunting question of Ilsa's last minute betrayal is finally answered for Rick. Ironically, upon learning the truth he is convinced that she is lost to him forever. He must console himself with memories of their brief interlude and the happiness of their last breakfast together.

How enchanting that last meal had been, sitting in an outdoor cafe, the soft strains of "their song" playing in the background. The innkeeper, seeing the looks that passed between the two lovers, miraculously produced a bottle of fine champagne from keep in his wine cellar. In the milk June morning creamy omelets laced with brie appeared steaming in front of them. Fresh buttery brioche, the fragrance of their recent baking still in the air, were topped with dabs of last season's strawberry-peach jam. With the threat of the advancing army a final toast to the future was all that they could manage before the sounds of the approaching guns forced them to part.

Café au Lait

There is nothing quite like the rich aroma and flavor of freshly brewed coffee. Grown in the hot moist areas of the world it has almost universal appeal. Although there are many different types of coffee the French are famous for their strong brew which is served with hot milk in the morning.

French roast coffee
hot milk

Freshly brew 2 cups of coffee. Heat 2 cups of milk. To serve, pour coffee and hot milk into each cup at the same time.

Brie Omelet

The pungent flavor of ripe brie adds a distinctive flavor to this creamy omelet. We suggest removing the outer rind of the cheese before cooking it but it is certainly edible under other circumstances.

3   eggs
3   tablespoons water
2   tablespoons butter
2   ounces ripe Brie

Whisk egg, water, salt, and pepper until frothy. Melt butter in an omelet pan over high heat. Tilt the pan to coat the surface with butter. Pour eggs into pan. When set begin to lift the edges here and there to let uncooked eggs flow under to pan surface. Lower heat. When eggs are almost completely cooked, add sliced brie to one half of the omelet, fold over and continue cooking for a few more minutes until the cheese is melted. Serve at once.

Petite Brioche

This is an American version of the classic French brioche. We offer this recipe because of its relative ease of preparation. Baked in four-ounce fluted molds, these rolls more closely resemble the traditional brioche. However, they may be baked in muffin tins. If, by chance, there are any rolls left over, they can be wrapped in foil and placed in the freezer. To serve again, merely heat in a 350°F. oven in foil for 15 minutes.

2	tablespoons warm water
½	package (one teaspoon) active yeast
3	tablespoons butter
1	egg
1	egg yolk (reserve egg white)
2	tablespoons sugar
⅛	teaspoon salt
1¼	cups sifted all-purpose flour
1	teaspoon sugar for glaze

Place yeast, water, salt, and 2 tablespoons sugar in mixing bowl. Stir until the yeast dissolves. Let stand for five minutes.

Stir in butter, egg, egg yolk, and ¾ cup of flour. Beat with a wooden spoon for 10 minutes or if using an electric mixer 3 minutes at medium high speed. Add remaining flour and mix thoroughly. Dough will be soft. Cover and let dough rise in warm, draft free place for 2 hours. Stir down and cover with plastic wrap. Chill in refrigerator overnight.

To bake preheat oven to 375°F. To form brioche, cut off ¼ of dough and set aside. Divide remaining dough into six portions. Place one ball in each well greased cup. Using dough set aside form six small balls. Wet finger and make a small indentation in the center of each larger ball. Place a small ball in each of the depressions. This will produce the characteristic topknot. Let rise in a warm place until double in bulk. Before baking brush with reserved egg white mixed with 1 teaspoon sugar.

Bake at 375°F. for 15 minutes or until golden brown.

Strawberry-Peach Jam

The natural flavor of homemade jam is well worth the effort it takes to prepare. This delicious combination of fruits gives you a jam not readily available in most stores.

1	pound fresh peaches
1	cup strawberries
1	ounce lemon juice
3	cups sugar
¼	bottle Certo

Peel, pit and crush peaches. (It will be easier to peel the peaches if you plunge them into boiling water for a few moments first.) Wash, hull, and crush strawberries.

In a heavy saucepan, combine fruit and sugar. Cook over medium heat and bring to a rolling boil. Boil 1 minute, stirring constantly. Remove from heat. Stir in Certo. Stir and skim for five minutes.

Pour into sterilized jars. Fill to within ½ inch of top. Seal with parafin.

INDEX